THE FAMILY FRAMEWORK

THE FAMILY FRAMEWORK

Essential Habits to Create Order, Joy, and Deep Connections at Home

BLAKE AND CHANDLER
ALLSMITH

Revell
a division of Baker Publishing Group
Grand Rapids, Michigan

Published by Revell
a division of Baker Publishing Group
Grand Rapids, Michigan
RevellBooks.com

Printed in the United States of America

Library of Congress Cataloging-in-Publication Data
Names: Allsmith, Blake author | Allsmith, Chandler author
Title: The family framework : essential habits to create order, joy, and deep connections at home / Blake and Chandler Allsmith.
Identifiers: LCCN 2025048662 | ISBN 9780800748043 paperback | ISBN 9781493455485 ebook
Subjects: LCSH: Parenting | Child rearing | Families
Classification: LCC HQ755.8 .A46165 2026
LC record available at https://lccn.loc.gov/2025048662

Cover design and illustration by Derek Thornton / Notch Design

Baker Publishing Group publications use paper produced from sustainable forestry practices and postconsumer waste whenever possible.

26 27 28 29 30 31 32 7 6 5 4 3 2 1

For our parents:
We stand on your shoulders.

For our children:
May our ceiling be your floor,
our best ideas be second nature,
and our worst ideas be hilarious stories.

CONTENTS

FOREWORD

Thirteen-plus years ago, I sat with my wife, Alyssa, in a Cracker Barrel in Ohio listening to a man named Jeremy Pryor tell me something I'd never heard before: A family was not supposed to be a random collection of individuals. A family was a *team*. Home was not a launching pad for the real life that happened out there somewhere in the future but *was* the real life and mission—right now.

Something rewired in me that night, and I've spent the years since trying to live it out in my own home. Somewhere along the way, in one of those weird small orbits of providence, I found out that Jeremy had already had this same conversation with a guy named Blake Allsmith.

Same epiphany. Same rewiring.

Blake and I became friends, and I learned he'd been on the same journey but was a few years ahead of me. In many ways, you're holding his reflections of that journey plus what Blake does best: distilling complex ideas into super bite-size, easy-to-activate truths that make you go, *Wow, I've never thought about that before.*

And that's why this book is going to be a massive treat to your family, just like the ideas in it have been to ours.

It's easy to highlight the things wrong with the Western family. (Truly, it is. Once you see it, you can't *unsee it.*) But it is much, much harder to answer the questions that follow: *Now what? How do I build the right thing?*

Blake has built that framework.

And he has earned the right to build it. He spent eight years running a venture-backed startup, raised millions of dollars, hired and fired people he loved, and then watched the whole thing compress down into a single sheet of paper in a coffee shop that paid off less than his credit card debt. He came home to four kids, a wife pregnant with number five, and no job. And instead of collapsing, he did something most of us would be too proud or too tired to do: He opened a Google doc and began to apply the leadership skills he'd learned to the one organization that actually mattered.

Five years, two more kids, and four more businesses later, he is not theorizing. He is reporting from the field as a real-life practitioner.

Clear leadership structure. Disagreement protocols that are more than just vibes or soft apologies. Family values that do not get laminated, hung in the entryway, and forgotten. A family mission. A vision for what you are actually building together. Goals. Rhythms. Traditions that shape your kids into the kind of adults you actually want walking out your door in fifteen years.

Genuinely, you will be blown away by the level of practicality in this book.

And if at first glance this all feels a touch corporate for your family, then hopefully you'll realize how far we've fallen. In no world should the most important team (families) be out-planned, out-strategized, or even out-funned (not a word, I know) by other, less important teams like businesses and sports.

Warmth and framework are not enemies. They are friends.

A framework is not a cage. It's a trellis. It's the thing the vine grows on so it doesn't collapse in the dirt.

What Blake has built is a trellis.

I will close with the thing I think about most when I think about families like Blake's and mine and, God willing, yours: Our job as parents is to make our ceiling our children's floor. To build greater levels of faith and love and impact through successive generations.

So open the door: Read this book.

Pick one practice.

Install it on Monday.

And then *keep going*.

Jeff Bethke
New York Times bestselling author

INTRODUCTION

Our Story

That's it? I don't understand."

My wife, Chandler, stood in the doorway of our home office with tears in her eyes, holding a sheet of paper that listed the terms we had just accepted to sell our business (Cladwell). After paying off debt, preferred investor shares, and legal fees, we'd barely make enough money to last us the rest of the year. This was not the Silicon Valley outcome we'd dreamed of. In eight years, we had gone through a lot after founding and leading a venture-backed, eight-figure tech startup, including:

- quitting my stable job when we had a six-month-old baby;
- going through our first two years with $0 pay, burning through all our savings;
- hiring (and firing) some of our dearest friends;
- leaving and renting out our house to make ends meet (and having baby #2 a month later);
- raising money from sixty-plus investors, totaling millions of dollars in venture capital investment;

- closing three separate rounds of funding on Christmas Eve;
- taking out personal debt against our home to make payroll (while having baby #3);
- moving our young family to San Francisco and then Los Angeles, while also renting out our home on Airbnb to make ends meet;
- attending 500 Startups accelerator eighty-plus hours a week with three kids under five;
- working with the world-class investors who scaled Dollar Shave Club, Liquid Death, and MeUndies;
- scaling to a team of thirty-plus people building complex technology together (while having baby #4);
- spending weeks on the road to close deals with Nordstrom, Macy's, and other major retailers; and
- navigating a grueling and emotional sale process, losing friends and advisers along the way.

All that sacrifice boiled down to a measly sheet of paper with a dollar amount less than our credit card debt. My wife, who had sacrificed alongside me for eight years, had tears rolling down her freckled face as she looked at me with a mix of disappointment and confusion.

My stomach dropped as waves of shame and guilt washed over me. Thoughts raced through my mind. *How did we end up here? Have I sacrificed my family's well-being for a failed dream?* The weight of letting down the people I loved most was almost unbearable.

In the fall of 2019, I became jobless, teamless, and without any prospects. But what we lacked in money and opportunities, we made up for in children—our fifth was due in two months. Chandler and I went to a coffee shop, and I opened a blank document on my laptop to write out a plan. We needed to figure out how to make money fast while also being present and homeschooling—all during the infant stage once again.

I thought the last eight years of running a business had been a crucible, but it turns out it was merely a training ground for what came after.

We were in a real pinch.

I've talked to a lot of fathers and mothers who were also in a pinch. Raising a family, especially a young family, is not for the faint of heart. Instagram makes it look shiny, meaningful, and light, but anyone who has been in the arena knows it can take everything out of you. You must create security and routine for a young household. You must support and encourage your equally exhausted spouse. You must teach and nurture little ones, helping them learn right from wrong. You must unite people with sometimes competing agendas. And, yes, you must create income to fund it all.

So, what do you stand to benefit from reading this book? Maybe you're thinking about starting a family, or maybe you're in a "dark night of the soul" like we were. Do you carry the heavy weight of needing to provide, lead, and somehow also connect at the same time? Are you and your partner on the same page? Do the competing demands feel overwhelming? I hear you. Our plan for this book is to present a simple framework that you can implement to help your family thrive in every way, from relationships and direction to consistency and order.

How We Learned to Thrive

As Chandler and I stared at the blinking cursor on my laptop, we started frantically listing what we needed to do. We obviously needed to figure out a plan for money. We also had a big, growing family, and we couldn't just ignore the kids. We were DONE with "dividing and conquering"; we wanted to *actually* work as a team. We needed a new vision that could realistically bless our family—no more bait-and-switch with sacrificing today for billion-dollar dreams in the future. We needed to figure out how to gain traction toward all of this, while also being in the newborn phase again.

As we wrote everything out, it started to feel familiar. I had faced a lot of adversity as the CEO of a young company. It was pretty common to look at overwhelming situations, map out our priorities, and then go "head down" and execute.

My family needed me to use the leadership skills I'd learned at work and bring them home. Now, five years later, I want to share with you what worked (and didn't work) for us. In corporate life we'd call this a **framework**: a flexible system to help an organization achieve its goals. And that's what we did.

We prioritized our marriage. Even with very little money, we committed to a weekly date night, relying on family and friends to help us with the kids.

We got on the same page. We took a trip (just the two of us) and mapped out our mission, vision, and values. Then we returned home and shared everything with the kids.

We started a cadence of meetings. We planned daily, weekly, quarterly, and annual meetings to establish our priorities and track our progress.

We brought order into our home. We budgeted, established a healthy rhythm, and developed systems for everyone in the family. We also invested in meaningful traditions we all enjoyed.

And *we honestly started to thrive*—individually, as a family, in business, and even in our wider community. Chandler and I collaborated to create goals for healthier habits, and we discovered a weekly rhythm that we actually enjoyed. For the first time ever, we followed our budget without feeling deprived. We even found time for hobbies we both enjoyed. I'm not sharing this to say, "See how great we are!" but our life really started to look so much healthier.

Since then, we have:

- built four new businesses that more than provide for us and allow us to be together as a family;

- purchased and rehabbed a property together, cash-flowing it as a short-term rental;
- started homesteading together with vegetable gardens, chickens, and ducks;
- hosted gatherings each week in our home for our faith community;
- traveled as a couple and as a family across the country and internationally while homeschooling and working remotely;
- launched a homeschool co-op for our local community;
- learned new sports and hobbies together as a whole family; and
- welcomed babies #6 and #7.

And we did it all while feeling closer as a couple and a family than we ever had. Five years later, my worst fear of "failure" has turned into the greatest blessing in my life: a thriving family.

Of course, we're not perfect. (Our oldest is only thirteen, for goodness' sake.) I'm not trying to create some influencer image of perfection. But I can honestly say we share a deeper bond and achieve more together now than ever before, and the framework we share in this book is a major part of the why.

What Is a Framework?

A framework is simply a system for creating order. In business, we use frameworks (also called "playbooks") all the time for finances, operations, technology, marketing, sales, and so forth. It's a way of standing on the shoulders of the businesspeople who came before us and learning from them rather than reinventing the wheel. The mindset in business is there are brand-new, complex problems every day for your unique business. Why not do what most businesses do for the boring stuff and save your creativity for the things that really matter?

Take something as foundational as revenue, expenses, and profit. Rather than invent a new measure of health for every separate business, most executives embrace those numbers as good enough so they can focus on other, "bigger" problems. It's less about being rigid or unoriginal and more about freeing up energy to be creative where it counts.

I learned a lot from running a venture capital–backed startup for eight years. Managing thirty-plus people, raising millions of dollars, and serving millions of customers was definitely a master's course in leadership. I'm trying to bring those best practices (with hopefully less stuffy business jargon) here.

After selling my company, I naturally started searching for frameworks to help our family thrive. I read books on marriage, parenting, life design, conflict, running larger households, homesteading, personal finances, and more. Then I started documenting the systems that actually worked for our family, creating any necessary new ones, and forming it all into a cohesive framework.

Just to be clear, on the way to finding something that works, we tried a LOT of things that didn't work. Like *at all*. Like when I created a one-page, twelve-point font Standard Operating Procedure (SOP) for how to do the dishes for our kids. That lasted all of two days. Or like when we tried a new-age budgeting process that required us to "reward" ourselves by spending a fixed chunk of our monthly income to "attract" more income. That destroyed our budget. Or like when I thought it would be helpful to premake fifty vegan breakfast burritos so Chandler wouldn't have to make lunch for the quarter. That was so disgusting.

Lots of trial and error.

But after all that trial and error—along with a lot of patient but clear pushback from Chandler—we've landed on a minimal framework that has helped our family and the families around us thrive.

You might be thinking, *Can a framework really improve my family life without making it feel cold or transactional?* We had the same concern. But we found that when applied thoughtfully, our framework enhances our connections, reduces stress, and brings more joy into our home.

How and Why We Wrote This Book

Over time, we noticed that whenever we shared what worked for our family with our friends or on social media, people wanted to hear more. A couple thousand people started using our structure for weekly, quarterly, and annual meetings. We started getting requests to speak at marriage seminars or to family groups to share what was working and accrued tens of thousands of followers on social media and on my digital newsletter—not for business content but for content about *family*. And then these followers would come back and tell us that it actually worked! That felt really great and made us wonder if we should share our framework a little more formally.

After we put the first draft of this book together, we shared it with thirty families to test each chapter. They committed to try each practice within two weeks and provide feedback on how we could make it more accessible. That process was incredibly helpful, and I thank those families at the end of this book.

Most of this book is written in either the "we" voice or from my (Blake's) voice for simplicity. However, Chandler was deeply involved in every stage of development, writing, testing, and editing. Throughout these pages, you'll find her notes, offering her perspective when it differs from mine or brings additional insights.

> Hi—I'm Chandler!
>
> If you come to our home on the banks of the Ohio River, you'll probably be greeted by a barefoot child with a toothy grin holding some sort of animal.

That child will call out to the rest, and soon you'll have a pack of very loud kids welcoming you and ushering you inside as you try not to trip on the sea of shoes by the garage door. I'll say hello, give you a hug, and probably make you an espresso. Blake will hear the commotion from his office downstairs and come up to greet you as well. We'll head out to the garden or down to our riverfront, or I might just pull up a pile of laundry and start folding as we chat.

Our life here isn't simple. We have seven kids, and we homeschool them all. We live on fourteen acres that demand a lot of care and energy. We're deeply connected in our faith, learning, and entrepreneur communities in our city. We bring our older kids into our work and businesses. We have lots of extended family in town. We host large gatherings in our home every week. We produce e-courses and podcasts. We own and run long- and short-term rental properties and a growth marketing agency. (And we didn't think seven kids were enough living things to care for, so we added chickens, ducks, cats, and a dog to the mix.)

But with all that going on, we're honestly thriving. Our days are full of challenges—our kids fight like regular kids, business obstacles sometimes feel like a game of whack-a-mole, and there's often a toddler running around the house without pants—but we love the life we're building together. We like our kids and want to spend time with them (and I think they like us too). Our marriage is strong, and I'm more in love with Blake than I was when we got married seventeen years ago. We feel deep purpose and direction in our days.

This book is the product of about 750 weekly meetings, sixty quarterly off-sites, and fourteen annual vision retreats. It's the result of many failed experiments in our home and many great successes. It's weekly check-ins, lists of issues, Standard Operating Procedures (SOPs), trials and errors, and trials again. These tools allow us to manage and grow a complex, organic, beautiful life.

About 99 percent of the words in this book were typed by Blake, but I'll pop in every so often to share my perspective. We've processed, talked through, and lived every chapter together. This is a real and sometimes vulnerable peek into our life and the valuable lessons we've learned along

> the way. I hope these tools can serve your family and bring vision, clarity, unity, and harmony to the people in your care. May these pages equip you to build a beautiful life with the people you love.

We both believe that a child's experience of family will shape them more than anything else in this world. If we can reduce pain and promote thriving in families by just a little bit, this effort will be completely worth it.

How This Book Will Benefit You

Each chapter of this book is meant to provide a lightweight, simple system any family can implement within one week. We introduce the topic, walk through the exact process, and then share stories and tips from our own experience implementing the system. Every tool in this book is something Chandler and I have used in our family for multiple years and seen positive results from.

We've divided the framework into four main areas: Relationships, Direction, Meetings, and Operations. The reason we put them in that order is because I've found they build on one another. For example, if your marriage is struggling, it will be almost impossible to get on the same page for the big picture. If you don't know where you're going as a family, you won't be able to make meaningful progress through weekly meetings. And if you aren't having a cadence of regular meetings, then you'll have no way to know if the tools you're implementing are helping or burdening your family.

My recommendation is to read this book all the way through like a novel. I've tried not to make it too heavy with instructions so you can crank through it. After you have the big picture, pick the one tool that you think would make the biggest impact on your family and implement it.

You might want to start with a weekly meeting with your partner. Sound like a lot? Don't worry—we've got a simple structure you can use to hopefully cut down on those late-night chats about budget or who has which car tomorrow.

If a process ever starts to feel overly burdensome or unnecessary, we officially give you permission to drop it. Now, we're both a little type A, so we understand the pull to try to complete everything perfectly. But we promise no one is going to be grading you. Every family is different, and people change over time. Resist the temptation to do things just because others are doing them; only implement the minimal tools necessary to help your family thrive.

Our hope is that this book can be a starting point for a new era in your family's life. No matter the size of your family unit, the principles in this book are adaptable. We've seen families from all kinds of backgrounds apply these systems with remarkable results.

We hope you will come back to the systems again and again for years to come, customizing and building on them in ways that uniquely bless your family.

Thanks for checking out this book. Now, let's get started!

CHAPTER 1

The Power of a Framework

If you're reading this book, you're likely motivated, good-hearted, and intelligent. And I'm guessing that leading your family feels really hard— maybe harder than it's supposed to be.

You are not alone. This is the experience of many families in the West today: supercapable, good-hearted, diligent people trying really, really hard yet barely surviving, often ending up completely exhausted or failing altogether.

But there is a better way.

How a Framework Can Help Your Family

I love this quote from business theorist, composer, and economist W. Edwards Deming: "A bad system will beat a good person every time."[1]

I don't know about you, but sometimes I feel like I just choose to do life on "hard mode" (says the parent who homeschools their seven kids and runs four businesses). Rather than embrace a simple system, I just try harder. But the secret to most things is not being profoundly diligent or skilled—it's just finding a framework and submitting to it.

When you embrace a framework, you automatically opt in to some massive benefits:

- **Compounding.** The truth is, most of your responsibilities in your family have been solved for millennia: food, clothing, shelter, training, discipline, family harmony, and so on. Rather than starting over and trying to figure it all out yourself, you can draw wisdom from those who came before you in family, business, organizations, and leadership and embrace what has worked for others.
- **Consistency.** Good parenting, in particular, is 90 percent consistency. I personally struggle with this, but when you embrace a system, consistency is built in. By trusting the system, you can stick to the process.
- **Clarity.** Once you put your problems into a system, you can see where your challenges lie. Rather than feeling like your entire life is a jumbled mess, you can locate specific issues and define them, which is more than half the battle.
- **Creativity.** Some problems in your family are brand-new or highly specific to your life. These will require immense creativity and ingenuity. By embracing a framework, you free up your problem-solving energy for the places it's needed most.

These four Cs (compounding, consistency, clarity, and creativity) are so important that they will outperform energy and raw talent every time. For example, my kids and I do Brazilian jiujitsu (a martial arts framework). Several times a month we'll see an insanely athletic person with no experience come into the gym expecting to dominate everyone, only to be beaten by a sixty-year-old grandmother with a brown belt. Frameworks have leverage—they make hard things easier.

So, why don't we have frameworks for families in the West? If frameworks are so great, why don't most families already use them? Great questions.

Where Did All the Family Wisdom Go?

Throughout recorded human history, families have maintained cultures that pass along wisdom from generation to generation—values, habits, recipes, and systems. These are generally called *traditions*. But in the West, and in the past century in particular, traditions have dwindled at an alarming rate.

That's because the modern nuclear family is actually a very recent experiment. By "modern nuclear family," I mean a home where Dad (and most likely also Mom) leaves for work; kids leave for school, sports, and activities starting at age four; and everyone reconvenes in the evening to recover and prep for the next day. The home (and family) is a place of recovery from your individual life—not a place of life itself. Grandma and Grandpa are retired in Florida, while aunts, uncles, and cousins live wherever the heck else (and are likely *not* on the same page as you are as a parent). Family is a loose affiliation for leisure at best.

This is new. And on literally *any* measure you can imagine—divorce rates, child education levels, parental and child mental health, long-term connection between family members—it's a complete and total failure. In the words of Wendell Berry,

> The modern household is the place where the consumptive couple do their consuming. Nothing productive is done there. Such work as is done there is done at the expense of the resident couple or family, and to the profit of suppliers of energy and household technology. For entertainment, the inmates consume television or purchase other consumable diversion elsewhere.[2]

Throughout human history, family was less about optimizing individual self-interest and more about thriving as a multigenerational team. If you weren't a cohesive unit, your family would literally die. Survival was a collaborative effort, and maintaining both your immediate and extended family was the primary strategy for staying alive. The grandparents depended on the next generation to care for them as they aged, and in return, they coached the parents and helped raise the young children. Aunts, uncles, and cousins teamed up and pooled their resources. Mother and Father worked together on the land with their children in eyesight, and as soon as the little ones were old enough to walk, they joined the cooperative game of "Don't starve and don't get pillaged." We're wired for this level of teamwork and connection to be the core center of meaning in our lives. When we operate this way, there's a natural passing down of best practices to survive and thrive from generation to generation.

Then came the Industrial Revolution. Dad (and more recently Mom) began to gain a lot of identity from the work done away from the home. This work-world wasn't a place for children, so the kids needed to find a new team and identity among their peers.

Now, to be fair, this new state of being has brought some major advancements in freedom, such as greater career access (especially for women), the ability to live where you want, and more autonomy to design your own life. But we've gone from being a team to being a collection of individual roommates. And if you're like me, it's hard to even imagine anything different. Along with losing meaning and connection, we've lost our compounding wisdom of how to operate as a family.

That's why it feels like you're living on hard mode. You are trying to do it all yourself, from scratch—and that's hard. But you're doing the best you can.

The Family as an Organization

Since I started writing this book, I have spoken to numerous parents about how they raise their families, and I've learned one exciting fact: Families of all shapes and sizes are discovering, inventing, and implementing systems to help their families thrive.

In May 2024, *The New York Times* published an article titled "Honey, I Love You. Didn't You See My Slack About It?"[3] It details how venture capital investor Ben Lang created a complex Notion doc to optimize his and his wife's household and relationship. In this document, he captured everything from special memories to grocery lists to vacation plans. Lang also recorded insights about their personality types and love languages. The document template went viral, being downloaded countless times as it obviously struck a chord with many readers.

I've heard stories about people like Denis Beauséjour, a retired Procter & Gamble vice president–turned-pastor. He and his wife fund an annual retreat for their kids and grandkids where Denis leads sessions on the family's goals. They discuss individual and collective aims and make lists of values, and throughout the year they hold regular check-ins to stay accountable.

Another example is my friend Lucas, the president of a large video agency. He wrote SOPs for his eight children to follow to make breakfast each morning. After I told my kids about it, we decided to drive over and see for ourselves. At 6:30 a.m., we sat in their kitchen. The kids, ages two to twelve, worked together to set the table and make chorizo, scrambled eggs, and coffee—all while their parents slept. Once they had finished, the parents walked in together to sit and enjoy the meal with their kids. The homemade breakfast was better than what you'd find at a nice brunch place, and they have it *every day*. And his kids are so proud.

What do these leaders all have in common? They took what they had—often organizational tools—and applied it to their families to help them thrive. They used their work or leadership skills to propel their families to where they want to go.

This phenomenon is particularly common in the entrepreneurial community. But where did the idea come from? Something is happening generationally in the USA, so let's explore this further.

In 1989, Stephen Covey's *The 7 Habits of Highly Effective People* focused on personal and professional development for individuals. Covey later expanded these concepts to families in *The 7 Habits of Highly Effective Families*, where he introduced the idea of a family mission statement and emphasized its power:

> A family mission statement is a combined, unified expression from all family members of what your family is all about—what it is you really want to do and be—and the principles you choose to govern your family life. It's based on the idea that all things are created twice. First comes the idea, or the mental creation; then comes the reality, or the physical creation. It's drafting the blueprint before constructing the building, writing the script before performing the play, creating the flight plan before taking off in the airplane. It's like the carpenter's rule: "Measure twice, cut once."[4]

What's most interesting to me is that families have been teaming up and accomplishing things for millennia, but only in the past two or three decades have some families begun to formalize this process. Why?

First, "soft" leadership tools—mission, vision, values, documented processes, cultural practices, meeting cadences—have become more widely used. As companies grew in size, we saw a change in organizational management from a traditional hierarchical structure to more modern approaches that emphasize company culture, employee empowerment, and strategic alignment. A big driver of this shift was the complexity in larger corporations that arose post–WWII.

But why are we starting to see these same tools now being applied to families? For that, we need to look at sociology. We're seeing a shift away from the hyperindividualism of Boomers and Gen Xers toward the more communal, family-oriented mindset of Millennials. Sociologist Gabriel B. Grant says, "Trends toward individualistic values are leveling off or reversing between the years 1980 and 2000. And, an unprecedented interest in purpose is emerging over the same time period."[5]

Effectively, Millennials are taking the Boomers' tools of business and using them on the organizations from which they derive deeper meaning—specifically, the family.

Can (or Should) You Run a Family Like a Business?

Why do we see this phenomenon in the entrepreneurial community? I think it's actually pretty simple: This is where Millennials have had leadership positions over the past two decades. The Mark Zuckerberg generation has seen a significant increase in young people leaving corporate jobs to start their own companies. As these entrepreneurs have had to learn how to lead their businesses in real time, they've taken those same skill sets home and applied them there.

This is my story as well. When our first son was born, thirteen years ago, I began to feel a tension between my personal ambition of working at a hedge fund and my desire to tuck my son into bed every night. That was when I stumbled across the writings of entrepreneur and lay pastor Jeremy Pryor. In his book *Family Revision*, Pryor talks about the juxtaposition between a modern and classical family's view of work:

> Today modern corporations have done much to provide a sense of team spirit, where a man feels he is leading or is part of a corporate team, with the primary identity of employee of the corporation. But a classical father could never view work in this way. He is already on a team and he is working for his family, no matter what type of job he has.[6]

I was inspired. What if all the leadership skills I'd developed in my career were primarily intended for my family? This concept captured my energy and imagination thirteen years ago in a way nothing else has. After reading Pryor's book, I quit my job. I wanted to become an entrepreneur, not for personal ambition but for my family. I aimed to merge my two worlds, and I immediately applied everything I learned in my startup at home (and often vice versa).

The freedom I've felt from breaking down the barrier between my "work self" and home life has been incredible. Especially with the recent increase in the ability to work from home plus increased flexibility, this is becoming more accessible for many families. Personally, I feel less tension regarding work-life balance because the ambitions and meaning in my home rival (and sometimes dwarf) those of my entrepreneurial career. The results have been more energy, deeper meaning, and greater connection in my home—and more integration of my whole self in my work.

This is the potential that *The Family Framework* sets out to find: integrating our work and family identities. We apply our ambition and operational skill sets to our partners and children to help them achieve and thrive as a group.

> I have a confession to make: When Blake first started talking about business tools like creating a mission statement and SOPs for our family, I thought it was kind of silly. Actually, just lame. I don't have a background in business or entrepreneurship, and my understanding of a mission statement was silly corporate logos that companies put on swag mugs but don't actually shape or influence anything. My idea of family was more organic—I didn't want schedules or goals imposed on our little budding family. But here's what I told my cute, very naive twenty-four-year-old self:
>
> 1. Your partner wants to invest in your family—let him. Blake is not you, and he's going to do things differently than you would. Do you believe he loves this family? (Absolutely.) Let him bring all his gifts and talents to the table. Your family needs his leadership and vision.

2. What do you have to lose? Literally, the very worst-case scenario is our family experiments with these systems for a few months and we hate them. If there's no fruit after a while, you can always stop, and there's no harm done.

I decided to lean in to the systems and framework Blake was proposing, and almost immediately I started to see the fruit. I began to experience the momentum of setting goals that would benefit our family and making progress toward them each week. Blake and I started dreaming together about what our family could be and do. Today these systems have become second nature. They have brought order and clarity, as well as space for joy and spontaneity even as our lives have become more and more complex. I'm so grateful that Blake was patient with my youthful eye-rolling and that he pressed into creating structure in our family.

Taking a Framework Too Far

Any good thing can be taken too far, and a framework is no different. I think it's pretty easy to imagine someone taking a good desire for order and squelching the spontaneity, joy, and relational meaningfulness from what makes family special. Here are four tips from our own experience to help ensure you don't take your family framework too far:

- **Do one thing each week.** A good rule of thumb is don't make more than one organizational change per week. This will keep your family from getting overwhelmed or overburdened.
- **Ask for feedback.** Continually ask your spouse and your kids, "Is this still working?" We'll cover this more in chapter 5 when we discuss radical candor, but it's all-important to get feedback from everyone in your family and optimize for a great experience for all of them.

- **Focus on high-leverage opportunities.** Rather than going through every system like a checklist, you're better off looking for the most challenging areas in your life and implementing new systems there. If you try to do everything at once, you'll lose steam before you do the things that matter most.
- **Make it your own.** Over time, you have to make your family framework your own. My recommendation is to start by copying the ideas in this book but feel free to edit and improve to match your needs.

Most of all, remember this system is meant to serve your family—your family is not meant to serve this system. If you keep that at the forefront of your mind, you'll do great.

AREA 1

RELATIONSHIPS

You're ready to systematize your family's life. Let's talk about . . . relationships?

Not very system-y, I know. However, this is where you have to start. **In any organization, the relationships within the team set the ceiling for relational health across the board—and relational health is the number one contributor to success.**

I'm an entrepreneur, so bear with me while I talk about startups for a second. Statistically, the number one reason any new company fails is cofounder conflicts (or issues with the founding team). Similarly, for families in the United States, between 35 and 50 percent of first-time marriages end in divorce.[1] If you list the potential risks to damaging your family or your business, the top existential threat is the relational health of the people who founded it.

In 2012, Google conducted a massive study called Project Aristotle to uncover how to create the perfect team. The research revealed that the number one factor of "enhanced teams" was "psychological safety," when "everyone feels safe in taking risks around their team members, and . . . won't be embarrassed or punished for doing so."[2]

That's why many companies and startups have created tools, vocabulary, and rhythms to ensure that the cofounding and team relationships thrive. These factors don't guarantee success, but neglecting them will almost certainly guarantee failure.

Cofounder "couples therapy" has become a booming industry in Silicon Valley as investors and entrepreneurs begin to see the importance of this central relationship.[3] Let me say it again: Investors and entrepreneurs spend *tens of thousands of dollars* on the cofounder relationship because they know it is the linchpin of a thriving organization.

Compare this with modern marriage. In America, we tend to think of marriage exclusively in terms of personal happiness and satisfaction. As long as the other person makes us happy, we stick it out. But as soon as we're no longer happy in the relationship, we bail. We Westerners see marriage primarily as a means of personal fulfillment. The logical outflow of this interpretation is that "working" on your marriage is either (a) an optional pursuit to make yourself happier or (b) a fruitless pursuit of a peripheral value (i.e., you can't attain happiness; it's always just over the horizon).

Imagine if people became cofounders for the same reasons that many of us get married. Picture Larry Page and Sergey Brin (Google's cofounders) sitting on a couch together, saying they just wanted to commit their lives to each other because it made them happy. Okay, that sounds nice, but the real reason they came together was because they had a vision to BUILD SOMETHING. They invested in their relationship *not* just to make themselves happy but primarily to serve the tens of thousands of people who work in their organization to fulfill a meaningful mission.

That's why I love thinking about marriage and family in terms of organizational health. It emphasizes the broader reality that your relationship with your partner impacts everyone in your care. Not just for your sake but for their sake, you *have* to create a thriving relationship.

> In general, most people lean toward one of two extremes. On one end, they (often women) can be more relationally focused—"How are we doing? How do our family dynamics feel? Is our relationship growing in depth and intimacy?" Or on the other end, they (often men) can be more outwardly focused—"What are we doing/creating/building in the world? What goals are we pursuing? What are we accomplishing externally?"
>
> It's easy to feel as if these leanings are in opposition to each other, like this is a zero-sum game where you can either have a happy, healthy relationship or get stuff done in the real world. But if your family is an active, thriving organization, both positions are deeply needed for the health and longevity of your team. Without relational health, who cares what you accomplish? Your family will not have the foundational glue to remain together long-term. But without a common purpose and goal, your family will have nothing outside itself to build toward. The tension between these positions is exactly what your team needs for long-term thriving. So lean in to it! Be grateful for your partner's differences. Their gifts are exactly what you need to build a beautiful, thriving family that will bless your community and the world for generations.

As we introduce these tools, it's essential to engage with them by asking not only, "How can this make me happy?" but also (and more importantly), "How can this help those I care about thrive?"

CHAPTER 2

Start with a Weekly Date Night

When we first started our company, my cofounder, Tim, and I established a weekly "date." Sometimes we took long walks and other times we played tennis and ate lunch together.

Why did we take two hours a week just to hang out and connect?

When you're head down, grinding and building a company, it's very easy to take your cofounder for granted. You communicate about work-related needs, but you start to forget that they are a person too. We had both quit our jobs and were living on savings as we built our business together. This stuff is stressful!

The same is true for building a family. What started as a vibrant romantic partnership can devolve into a transactional roommate dynamic. Nobody wants that, but it can be hard to prioritize the relationship amid all the competing demands. Shouldn't we invest as much time and thought into our primary relationship—our spouse—as we do into a cofounder?

Regular cofounder "date nights" are standard practice for many companies. There are a lot of different recommendations on how to do it, but here are several components that are almost always present:

1. **Regularly recurring.** It's typically a weekly event on the calendar, which removes the burden of having to remember to schedule it every time. It's already built in, so you plan other things around it. Another key reason to make something regularly recurring is that it establishes a maintenance rhythm to prevent future problems rather than being an "as needed" or "emergency" event. It's like going to the dentist: The best approach is to schedule regular checkups. If you only go when there's a problem, it's likely already too late.
2. **Over a meal.** Almost without exception, cofounder dates take place over lunch or dinner. Throughout history, sharing a meal has carried relational weight—the phrase "breaking bread together" reflects the intimacy that comes from eating together. Across cultures worldwide, sharing a meal reinforces a sense of oneness and community. Food brings us together in a way other things do not.
3. **Holistic.** The topics of conversation during the cofounder date need to be wide-ranging. You should talk about non-business things such as your personal life, family, health, dreams, and so on. These topics remind us of our shared humanity and offer an opportunity to acknowledge and enjoy each other as whole human beings, not just as contributors to the organization.
4. **Big picture.** It's really easy to lose perspective in the daily grind of running a company. Cofounder dates let you step back and remember the big picture: Why are we doing this? Where are we going? Who are we becoming? Dwelling on these questions all day can be paralyzing, but never asking them will make your efforts feel mundane and lead to burnout.

5. **Relational.** The final core element of the cofounder date is its interpersonal focus. We need to ask, How are we treating each other? Humans don't always work well together; despite good intentions, we will hurt each other from time to time. We must create space to check in, see how the relationship is doing, and address any issues.

This may seem like a lot to cram into a weekly lunch or dinner, but even covering just a few of these points is a great start. Your cofounder relationship—your marriage—is far too important to leave to chance. Your family must have a disciplined and consistent rhythm to maintain and improve the relationship between its cofounders.

Implementing a Weekly Date Night

Let's dive into the practice specifically for the home: the weekly date night. Chandler and I have been having a weekly date night for seventeen years. We began this tradition even before I started my company because my father gave it as his number one piece of advice for maintaining a healthy marriage. (Must give credit where credit is due, so thanks, Dad!)

It sounds like such a simple thing to make happen, but man, it's easy to skip when family life gets busy. Here are some ideas to help you make it happen:

1. **One owner.** There is a concept in economics called the "tragedy of the commons." It means when everyone shares ownership of something, no one owns it at all. If you don't want to neglect date night, you have to choose an owner whose job it is to ensure it happens. Sure, you could alternate each week, but that's one more thing to track. Here's my personal opinion: Make it the husband's job. Here's why: In most households (even with dual-income earners),

the wife bears more of the mental load for the day-to-day of the home.[1] Let's not give her one more thing to plan. I strongly believe someone has to own date night, and I prefer it be the husband, but do whatever works best for your relationship.

2. **Same time every week.** As with cofounder dates, removing the scheduling burden will make your date more likely to happen. If you need someone to watch your kids, you can schedule a recurring time with a family member or sitter each week. If you truly consider the date to be of the utmost importance, you don't want to let it get drowned out when life inevitably gets busy. If something comes up and you have to cancel, reschedule it for the same week. Just commit that you won't let a week go by without some sort of date night.
3. **Side-by-side time.** A good date night starts with side-by-side time, which means doing a shared activity such as taking a walk or hike, going to an art exhibit, playing a game, or biking. This may be a guy thing, but I find it easier to connect when I'm next to someone doing something (versus sitting still across a table). I can easily forget myself and open up more naturally this way. It's good to have a couple options in mind for outdoors and indoors if you live in an area with distinct seasonal changes. Our defaults are a long walk in the summertime and a quick workout at the gym in the wintertime.
4. **Face-to-face time.** After side-by-side time, you need to have face-to-face time over a meal. For the same reasons I stated previously, sharing a meal deepens your connection with your spouse. It doesn't need to be a huge romantic dinner at an expensive restaurant; it can be a simple picnic or whatever suits your budget.
5. **No "operations" talk.** Topics like budget, calendar/scheduling, and specific behavior issues are generally off-limits

for date night. If it's urgent or emotionally heavy, address it briefly, but otherwise save those conversations for your weekly business meeting. (We typically have our date night within forty-eight hours after our weekly meeting, so we have a clean slate.)

6. **Topics/questions to discuss.** This might sound kind of nerdy, but I like to have some go-to questions or topics prepared for date night. I love talking with my wife, but even as an extroverted external processor, I sometimes need a little help to keep the conversation flowing. I often search online for "date night questions," and I also bookmark things I come across on social media or in newspaper articles that I want to hear Chandler's thoughts on. Here are some of our go-to conversation starters and recurring topics:
   - Tell me about what you're reading these days.
   - Anything on your heart or mind lately?
   - Tell me about something you felt this past week that you wouldn't tell anyone else.
   - How do you think we're doing?
   - Is there anything I can change or do differently to improve your life?
   - Let's imagine what life will be like in twenty-five years.
   - I'd love to hear your thoughts on this quote, tweet, article, and so on.
   - Can you tell me about when you were __ years old? What were you like?
   - (If applicable) How do you feel like you're doing spiritually? What about our family?

> For likely obvious reasons, this is one of my favorite rhythms in our relationship: a few hours carved out each week to be together, talk about the things on our minds, and share the things we don't share with anyone else. Sometimes the dates are really memorable, but most

of the time they're simply consistent points of connection that happen once a week, every week.

These moments add up to hours and hours of relational intimacy that keeps our hearts joined together even when the rest of life feels busy.

Tips for Date Night

Here is an assortment of tips Chandler and I have compiled based on our seventeen years of experience:

- **It doesn't have to be fancy.** Some of our favorite date nights were when we had very little. We were early in starting our company and paying ourselves nothing, so date night consisted of a split Chipotle bowl and a walk. To be totally honest, those dates were just as meaningful—if not more so—than when we've had or spent more. It's the connection that matters most, not the amount of money spent.
- **You will probably fight sometimes.** For a long time, about one in every eight of our date nights would end up in some sort of difficult conversation or argument. That's okay! Fighting on some date nights is normal, and it's a sign you've created space for a meaningful (though perhaps uncomfortable) conversation to happen. Now, if you're consistently arguing on more than a quarter of your date nights, or if you can't seem to stop bickering in general, I recommend seeking marriage counseling. Over time, constant conflict will wear you down. However, if it happens less often than one in four times, I'd consider that healthy and productive.
- **Have a default location.** Sometimes you just don't know what to do this week for date night. When that happens to us, Chandler and I have our default: We eat sushi at

Ichiban in Mount Lookout and then take a walk around the Hyde Park neighborhood while eating ice cream. We've had this date fifty or more times. The servers all know us well—they know where we like to sit and that we're going to ask for our sushi on the giant wooden boat. It's wonderful.

- **Find a recurring solution for childcare.** Ask a family member or babysitter to commit to coming weekly at the same time. If it's a high schooler, ask them to connect you with an alternate if they're ever unavailable. Once this rhythm is locked in, it's much better than scrambling every week. Here's a pro tip: If a sitter cancels last-minute (or irresponsibly), never hire them again. It is *not* worth hiring inconsistent help. Also, if you don't have family nearby or room in the budget for babysitters, consider swapping childcare with another couple every other week. This is a great solution that benefits everyone involved.
- **You don't *have* to have sex afterward.** Maybe it wasn't on your mind this exact moment, but let's be honest: It's on our minds a lot of the time. I think it's best to separate date night from sex in terms of expectations. Sometimes you have a challenging conversation while you're out. Sometimes you get home late. Sometimes all the kids are still awake. There are just too many variables to treat the whole date as foreplay. Remember, the primary purpose of the date is to bolster the core relationship at the center of the family.
- **Double dates aren't date night.** Double dates are great, and I really enjoy them. However, they are not date night. The purpose of a date night is to reinforce the core relationship in *your* family. So, if you're doing a double date, go for it and enjoy—just know you still have a date night to schedule for the week.

- **Movies are a special treat.** If there is a movie I'm dying to see, we may see it on date night. Spending time with just the two of us in a theater watching a movie together is so luxurious. However, it limits the date's connection time, so we make it the exception, not the rule.
- **Make some date nights alcohol-free.** Everyone has their own stance on alcohol, but Chandler and I have refrained from drinking for the past three years. Initially, I thought date nights would be less special or romantic without alcohol—that really was one of the biggest hesitations I had about cutting it out. However, now that our date nights are consistently alcohol-free, I've noticed multiple benefits:
  - We argue less often.
  - It's *much* cheaper.
  - We do more interesting things.
  - Our conversations have more depth to them.

  Now, we drank during fourteen of our seventeen years of date nights, so there's no judgment on drinking by any means. Still, I recommend trying a few alcohol-free dates and seeing how this change impacts the experience.
- **Do it no matter what.** There will be times when you're injured or grieving or postpartum. We've had date nights after tragedies. We've had (many) date nights with a weeks-old newborn in the carrier. We've had date nights after surgery. Keep the rhythm consistent (and your expectations realistic).

Date night has been one of the most important practices in the most important relationship in my life. I believe in it, and I love it. For the sake of your children, your friends, and the other people under your care, please invest in this practice.

ACTION PLAN

Ready to benefit from the ideas in this chapter? Here are your three action points:

- Decide who owns date night.
- Find a day of the week that you both can make work at least 75 percent of the time.
- Schedule childcare for a month.

CHAPTER 3

Kid 1-on-1 Meetings

Let's talk about another major element of family life: your kids. Remember them? Whether you see them as colleagues, employees, or even little bosses, building connection with your kids is essential for your family to thrive. This tool has become one of my favorites now that I've found a better balance between work and family life.

As a fundamental rhythm for running teams, a 1-on-1 meeting is exactly what it sounds like: a private meeting between the team leader and a team member. We'll cover the structure of a weekly business meeting with your spouse in chapter 12, but in this chapter let's talk specifically about the weekly connection point with your children.

How to Have an Effective 1-on-1

The two behaviors that should always be present in a 1-on-1 are:

1. **Listening.** The leader asks questions and creates space for the team member to speak their mind, share their issues, and ask clarifying questions.

2. **Providing feedback.** The leader gives specific feedback for the benefit of the team member to help them grow.

My personal experience with 1-on-1 meetings started as a recipient. My first boss, Jim Bechtold, was an absolute *master* of this tool. Whenever I came into his office with a tactical question or needing a document, he would spin his chair away from his computer, place his hands in his lap, and ask me pointed questions like "How do you feel like your career is going?" or "How is your wife doing with her job?" Jim would ask multiple layers of questions, and he wasn't afraid to give me direct, candid feedback on my personal life, work habits, productivity, or anything else. Writing about it now makes me a little emotional. I think the reason he was so impactful is that he really did it for *my* good—not just because it was something he was "supposed" to do.

Later on, when I started running my own business, I knew that 1-on-1s needed to be a part of my regular rhythm. I tended to be a little more structured in how I ran my days, so I scheduled 1-on-1s with all my direct reports at the very beginning of the week. Every Monday I set aside thirty to sixty minutes for walking meetings with each person; I asked them what was on their mind, and then I shared what was on mine. In retrospect, I think I could have done more to keep these meetings from feeling sterile, but I believe the exercise was still incredibly important.

Whether you have 1-on-1s opportunistically or on a set schedule, I believe they are essential for any team to establish the following:

1. **Connection.** A team member's connection to the team is directly related to the strength of their individual relationship with the leader.
2. **Influence.** It sounds cheesy, but "They don't care how much you know unless they know how much you care" is a cliché for a reason. If you want to influence the direction and

culture of your team, you need to exhibit individual care for each team member.

3. **Clarity.** It is insane to me how you can tell a group of five people one simple thing, and they will come away with five different interpretations. If you want your team to be on the same page, you have to repeat yourself (both to the group and individually), ask for feedback, and clarify again. It's a constant task.
4. **Insight.** As a leader, you are *not* fully in touch with reality. You may have more big-picture context, but there are things hidden from you, and the only way to uncover them is through 1-on-1 conversations. Good leaders constantly mine their team members for perspective, wisdom, and feedback.
5. **Growth.** The only way for you to grow as a leader and for your team members to grow too is through uncomfortable moments of feedback. Both sides must embrace the need for honest input, recognizing that we rely on each other to tell us where we are off and humbly redirect our efforts.

Kid 1-on-1 Meetings

How can we bring the best elements of this business practice home? I've tried various iterations with my kids, and I'm sure I will keep experimenting for years to come. For now, I'll share what I'm currently doing and then some general tips to help you implement 1-on-1s with your kids.

For Kids 0–5

For Ford (newborn), Jojo (age two), and Imogen (age five), the formula is pretty simple: I get on the floor with them and play whatever they want to play. With Imogen, we might just eat lunch together in my office and play for thirty minutes. To be honest, it's a little boring playing Calico Critters for thirty minutes, but I know it really matters to her. With Jojo, our time together often occurs while my wife is cooking dinner. The depth of our conversations isn't anything profound; I simply ask about their favorites (color, toy, friend) and if they have any questions for me about what happened that week or in general. Finally, I affirm them and make sure they know I think they're wonderful and I love them.

For Kids 6–9

For Truman (age seven) and Penny (age nine), I really like playing a game and having some unstructured conversation. I don't have much of a set agenda, but if they say something about a friend, sibling, or anything else, I might investigate and ask them to share more. This is also the prime age for inviting a kid to go to the grocery or hardware store with you. These 1-on-1s are actually the most ideal for me, as I've found the best conversations happen while we're riding side by side in the car. My number one goal in these conversations is to see the world through their eyes. *What is life like for them? What are they afraid of? What are they excited about?*

For Kids 10–13

For Charleston (age eleven) and Everett (age thirteen), I'm starting to have more structured 1-on-1 meetings, coming with some prepared questions and thoughts. I ask them about their relationships with their friends, siblings, and God, plus their internal dialogue and anything else on their mind. If we have lunch for an hour, they spend at least forty-five minutes talking. I want to know what's on their hearts, and I want them to see that I understand (or at least am trying to). I also ask for their feedback on what I could do differently in our relationship. During the last fifteen minutes, I might share something on my mind that I've observed about them. It could be positive feedback like, "It made me so happy when I saw you protect your brother the other day," or it could be advice for a struggle I saw: "I noticed you lost your temper a couple times in the past week. Can I share with you how

I work to control my temper?" I've only been doing this level of kid 1-on-1 for two or three years, but they are some of my favorite moments of my week. I feel like I'm developing the beginning of lifelong friendships with these amazing people.

For Kids 14–18

I reached out to a couple mentors for this one, since my oldest is just now entering this age range. The biggest difference I've heard is that in the teen years you can start encouraging your kids to set personal goals while you serve as an accountability partner. For example, if your teenager says they really want to get better at playing the guitar, that's a personal goal. Write it down, help them map out the steps they need to take to improve, and ask for permission to check in each week. The key is the goal must be something *they* want; that way, you can be the coach, helping them learn how to direct themselves toward what they want in life.

For Kids 19+

I can draw upon my own experience with my father here. Early in my career, Dad and I had a weekly lunch together where we would catch up and chat about whatever we were reading or experiencing, and I would ask for advice. The key to this new-adult phase is backing off the accountability you provided in the teen years and serving as more of a sage than a coach. There's a grandfather I know who schedules monthly check-ins with each of his sons and daughters-in-law. He just asks them how they're doing and what he can do to help. (Note to future self!)

How Often Should These 1-on-1s Happen?

Ages 0–5: Opportunistic, child-led playtime every one to two weeks.

Ages 6–9: Opportunistic playtime, scheduled errands, or game time with child-led conversation every one to two weeks.

Ages 10–18: Weekly scheduled meal or snack with adult-led, prepared questions and feedback.

Ages 19+: Weekly meal or phone call to share whatever is on both of your minds.

> While having a scheduled 1-on-1 with each kid works great for Blake, I find it easier to focus on organic connections with our kids. I'm at home with them most of the time—often with a baby on my hip—and certain chores or activities I do with each child have become regular connection points.
>
> One of my daughters loves to cook. She really comes alive in the kitchen, so I invite her to help me prep dinner a few nights a week while the younger kids watch a show. Another daughter loves to organize things (weird, I know), so if I have to put some order to the chaos in a closet, I'll ask for her help. Her heart just opens up during these moments, and we talk about whatever is on her mind. Other kids love walking in the woods or digging in the garden with me. These everyday activities I'm already doing that spark each child's interest have become natural 1-on-1 connection points.

Tips for Meetings

Here are some tips I've learned from implementing kid 1-on-1s over time. Hopefully, they will save you from making the same mistakes I made along the way.

- **Make it special but not *too* special.** For example, I'll let them have a seltzer or small can of caffeine-free soda. If I'm on an errand, I might let them get a piece of candy or gum. In the past I tried to make these 1-on-1s full-on dates, where the kid got to choose the activity and we did something extravagant. That ended up backfiring big time—it was so much work that I did it less often, and the kids became entitled and jealous about what their special thing would be. Just a little bit of special turns out to be just right.

- **Share what you like.** Few things have been more fulfilling for me as a father than sharing the hobbies and interests I love with my children. My two oldest sons and I like to talk about entrepreneurship, jiujitsu, and wakeboarding together. My oldest daughter and I play or talk about music together. I think our culture is really child-centric, with most parents not wanting to "force" kids to adopt their hobbies. But there is a difference between *forcing* your kids to do something and *sharing* it with them. If the two of you share a hobby, it can be a connection point for life—so why deny them that opportunity if they're interested?
- **Do it discreetly.** Don't make a big demonstration of a particular 1-on-1 in front of the other kids. Siblings naturally get jealous, so it's best to subtly invite a kid out without drawing unnecessary attention. Also coach your kids to not make a big deal of it in front of their siblings. Yes, siblings need to learn how to handle jealousy, but it also can be minimized or avoided if handled the right way to begin with.
- **Five minutes is fine.** A quick connection is better than nothing. If all you can manage is a five-minute walk after dinner or a brief chat while washing dishes together, do it. Relationships are one long conversation, and the little connection points are just as necessary as the big ones.
- **Plan big trips.** Many parents wonder how often they should do bigger events. Right now, our default is every five years. When one of our kids has a fifth or tenth birthday (and later fifteenth and maybe twentieth), Chandler and I take them on a special trip to a national park. We got this idea from our friends Andrew and Rachel Peters, and it's been really special and enjoyable for all of us. I also try to take a kid with me whenever I travel out of town. This has been *plenty* for us,

and even if we didn't do the five-year trips, I honestly think it would be fine to have just an afternoon with Mom and Dad.

- **Use conversation cards.** Some of my kids don't need any help talking, but others need to be drawn out. I like to keep a pack of *The Ungame* cards in my car in case our conversations need a little help. Each card has a personal question like "What makes you most happy?" or "What's your favorite part of the week?" I got this idea from my mentor, Jeremy Pryor, and if there is ever an awkward silence, I'll pull out a card to keep the conversation going.

Hopefully these tips will help you get started with 1-on-1s with your kids. I've found these meetings to be something I really enjoy, and I can't imagine life without them now.

ACTION PLAN

The important thing is to manage your kid's expectations. Rather than schedule something recurring right away, start trying different things to see what works. Only make it regular when you know you can keep it up.

- Try a 1-on-1. (Remember, keep it simple.)
- Did it feel sustainable? If so, maybe repeat it. If not, try something different.
- Once you find something that you *like* to do and *can* do each week, *then* make it recurring.

CHAPTER 4

Who's the CEO?

Oh boy. We're going to talk about roles and hierarchy in the family. But before you throw this book out the window and cancel me to kingdom come, please hear me out. I truly believe this is worth exploring for the thriving of your family.

In my business career, one of the first things an investor would clarify when engaging with my cofounder and me was, "Who is going to be the CEO?" Selecting the CEO is one of the most foundational questions in starting any organization. Just who will be the leader?

According to a study published in the *Harvard Business Review*, between 1996 and 2020, 95 percent of the companies listed in the S&P 1200 and Russell 1000 had a singular CEO.[1] On a wider scale, the vast majority of all humans who have ever existed did so under a single leader at the top. As a species, we've lived under authority—the head of the tribe, the head of the multigenerational family, and the head of the family itself. Our species embraces organizational hierarchy by nature, almost without exception. Even primates as a whole thrive in a hierarchy.

However, despite our long history of thriving within hierarchies, people are increasingly uncomfortable with the idea of leadership structure in the home in twenty-first-century America. I think most homes actually do have a leader—father, mother, or even child—but we say there is no leader (or there's joint leadership) because it sounds nicer.

I've tried joint leadership. And it went horribly wrong.

When we started our company in 2012, my cofounder and I were uncomfortable with having just one leader. We had been friends for five years, and neither of us really wanted to be each other's boss—and we sure as heck didn't want the other to be our boss. I remember meeting with investors, successful executives, and advisers, and they all told us we *needed* to choose a leader.

The problem was that it started to get uncomfortable as soon as we broached the topic. I remember trying to talk through it on long walks or whiteboarding out different organizational charts, and the moment someone's name was in the CEO slot, the other person wanted to erase it. We were young, we had egos, and neither wanted to have a "boss."

So, we decided on an elegant solution: co-CEOs. We would divide up the CEO role according to our natural inclinations. I would pitch, and he would oversee finances. He would oversee the product, and I would oversee marketing. Certain decisions, like strategy and vision, would be decided jointly.

We immediately felt relieved. We both had the top title and could keep our egos intact. We would buck the overwhelming data from the history of companies, governments, civilizations, and our species. What could go wrong?

It turned out *a lot* could go wrong. We soon discovered some fatal flaws in the co-CEO model, especially for our young organization:

1. **Slowness.** I remember an adviser saying, "Having joint decision-makers means you're committing to being three

times slower than your competition." In my experience, this is true. We imagined that most of our decisions would be isolated, but it turned out that most of them were cross-functional. In terms of decision quality, it's so important to have joint *input*—and we had plenty of that—but after the joint input, someone needs to say, "Okay, I've listened to all sides of this, and we're going to do x." Often, a quick bad decision is better than a slow good decision because you can learn from your mistake and correct the course. Without the final-decision mechanism, my cofounder and I found ourselves in time-consuming debates that lasted until one of us gave in from exhaustion. Simple decisions that could have been made via email required lengthy meetings and discussions. The result? We delayed decisions. We accepted ambiguity. And we were *slow*. It took us eighteen months to launch our first product.

2. **Team confusion.** As we scaled the team, confusion increased. "Who do I go to for this decision?" became a regular request. Because we were continually redrawing the lines of who owned what, our team members were always behind in knowing the authority structure. This confusion typically had two results:
   - Some people moved ahead without any input.
   - Other people were afraid to make decisions out of fear of stepping on the wrong person's toes, so they did low-importance work.

   Creating clarity is the number one job of a leader. *What are we doing? How will we do it? Why do we do it?* We failed this task pretty royally.
3. **Relational tension and failure.** Eventually, what forced us to shift our structure was the relational tension our co-CEO model created. Because there was no final decision-maker, we would argue on and on until someone gave up. Those

> hours of debate aren't good for a cofounder relationship. It's better to just "disagree and commit" to supporting a decision to keep moving forward, but we didn't have a mechanism other than losing the argument or getting too tired to continue. Over time, this dynamic shifted our relationship from a deep friendship to one of mutual criticism. Even if I won an argument, I knew he hoped he'd be proven right and that we should have gone with his solution. Eventually, we stopped arguing and grew cold. Months later, he asked if he could leave to start another company. He did, and it was a significant loss to our original organization. We had been partners and friends, and neither of those things were ever fully restored. It makes me sad writing this now, as we were incredibly complementary and had an extremely high capacity for success. Speaking for myself, my ego got in the way of being a great teammate. Years later, we reconciled and got back on good terms, but our relationship will never be the same as it once was. This experience is a haunting reminder that without a clear decision-maker, the relationship is forced to bear the pressure of every decision—a burden that can break even the strongest of bonds.

Before we move on to the application for families (which I'm guessing you're dreading), I want to quickly clarify what a CEO does. Without this context, you might think they are dictators—making *all* the decisions in the organization—but that couldn't be further from the truth.

What the Leader *Actually* Does

I remember an adviser once told me that my job as a leader was to make sure I was the dumbest person in the room. If I could recruit a team where everyone was smarter than me, give them clear direction, create an environment where they could collaborate freely, and remove any roadblocks, then the company would thrive. Let's break down each of these elements and how they apply to family.

1. **Recruit a team where everyone is smarter than you.** We don't do a lot of "recruiting" in our families, but the point still stands: You should be looking for the places where your spouse and children are smarter than you. That's not a threat to avoid—that's an asset. It's a sign you're building a great team. If there's nowhere you think your spouse or kids are smarter than you: heads up, you're a jerk.
2. **Give them clear direction.** As the leader, you have to constantly point to where the team needs to go. Each individual will only have a fraction of the big picture; your job is to incessantly rearticulate the goal. (You don't have to invent the direction in a vacuum; you just have to cheerlead it.)
3. **Create an environment where they can collaborate freely.** Remember that study from Google I mentioned earlier, on what matters most to build a high-functioning team? The number one ingredient is psychological safety.[2] As the leader, it's your job to create an environment where everyone feels safe enough to bring their best.
4. **Remove roadblocks.** As the leader, your job is to clear whatever stands in your teammates' way. Sometimes that means making peace between rivals, other times it's allocating resources so someone can move toward the goal. You're the white blood cell: constantly monitoring, ready to blast anything blocking your team.

As you can see, the job of the CEO is actually less about decision-making power (although this is an element) and much more about responsibility for outcomes, harmony, and clarity. Without a central owner, these key elements to an organization's thriving will suffer.

Who Is the Leader at Home?

Oh no. We're going there. (Relax—it'll be okay!)

Most modern families feel uncomfortable with the idea of having a central authority figure in the home. In the West, since the beginning of the nineteenth century, families have been moving steadily toward egalitarian parenting or even child-led households, where leadership is distributed equitably among all members.

I'm sure there are great arguments for having egalitarian parents or child-led homes where all roles are interchangeable, but this book is about how my wife and I have applied business practices and tools to our home. As we've already seen, egalitarian models don't work for most business organizations, so hear me out on our approach. Let's entertain the scary idea that each of our homes needs a "CEO" who is responsible for:

- Building a team smarter than the CEO.
- Creating clarity.
- Creating an environment of psychological safety.
- Removing roadblocks.

The challenge in front of you and your spouse is: Which of you will be the CEO? Aaaaaagh!

Take a quick breath. I'm not here to convince you that this is about gender or age, nor will I prescribe a specific structure for your family. I just want you to consider that *any* structure is better than *no* structure. Ultimately, only you and your spouse can make this decision for your family.

Here are the elements Chandler and I considered as we made our decision:

- **Capacity.** Over the past thirteen years, Chandler has been pregnant ten times and given birth to seven children. This has taken a huge toll on her body and energy. Given her waxing and waning energy levels, we thought it made sense not to have Chandler also be responsible for all CEO tasks.

- **Familiarity.** We both grew up with fathers who were the leaders in the home. We know what that looks like and had no reason to reject it.
- **Religion.** Chandler and I both adhere to the Christian faith. Christianity traditionally selects the father as the leader of the home. Modern Western Christianity debates this a bit more, but the traditional approach was most familiar to us.

I've heard people also take into consideration things like natural gifting, capacity for the home versus work outside the home, desire for the role, and so on. If you feel really stuck, just pick one person for ninety days and see how it goes. If you don't like it, switch roles and try that.

A note on child-led households: I'm going to go out on a limb and say this is a dumb name for the great idea of having empathy and understanding for your child. You can (and should) have empathy and understanding for your child, but putting them in a position of leadership over your family is about as smart as putting them in a position of leadership over your government, nonprofit, or business.

So You've Been Appointed Leader

Here are some tips for whoever is chosen to be the leader in your home:

- **Become a world-class CEO.** If you're the CEO, you owe it to your family to become as competent as possible. Read books, listen to podcasts, watch YouTube videos, and hire a coach. At the end of this book, you will find some resources to help you. Leadership is a weighty responsibility and should not be taken lightly.

- **Honor your team.** If your team trusts you enough to follow your lead for the good of the organization, you need to thank them regularly. Empathize with them. Listen when they disagree with you.
- **Ask for feedback.** Regularly ask your spouse and children for feedback on how you're doing. Continual improvement in this role is essential, and honest feedback from your direct reports is vital to make that happen.
- **Focus on self-improvement.** If you're going to lead your family, you must have your personal life in order. You need to be a trustworthy person. You must live up to your commitments. Be enjoyable to work with, be faithful, and be capable of caring for yourself and others. Go to therapy. Get a mentor. Get physically healthy. Pull yourself together for the sake of your family. Getting your own life in order will turn you into someone worthy of your family's trust.
- **Get a board of directors.** I have three people who serve as my "board," and if they agree on a significant decision in my life, I will do what they say. (In no particular order, they are Jeremy Pryor [my mentor], my dad, and David Barr [our counselor].) My wife knows she can also go to these people, and they will support us. As humans, we are incredibly delicate creatures. Mental health can go wrong. We can listen to bad advice. We can spend time with the wrong people. It is essential to have a trusted support system those in your care can appeal to.

It's easy to carry a lot of cultural baggage into this conversation. I have strong leadership abilities, and I've led teams and managed people most of my life. (Yes, I am the oldest child—you nailed it!) I can lead well, but I also know that leading comes with a heavy weight and responsibility. Leading well doesn't mean bulldozing your way forward and forcing people into your vision. It means putting yourself under the people you're leading by listening to them, internalizing what they need, asking for input, and ultimately taking responsibility for making hard decisions for the overall health and thriving of a team.

I feel so grateful to Blake for taking on the mantle of leading our family. He has purposefully and lovingly taken so much off my mental plate by laying down his life to serve our family through his leadership. He seeks out my opinions, welcomes my pushback, relies on my insights, and asks for my help. But he also is willing to say, "If there is something going wrong or something unhealthy in our family, I'm willing to take responsibility to make it right." I don't envy his position, but I am grateful for the way he loves me and our entire family by taking on this role.

ACTION PLAN

I recommend first answering these questions individually and then discussing them with your spouse.

- What did we feel when reading this chapter? (Or what do we feel when we hear the idea of establishing a leadership role in the family?)
- Who do we think is currently acting (whether sanctioned or not) as the leader in our family?
- Do you think we could decide on a leader for our family today? If not, can we decide on a process for making that decision? Or, if that's still too much, could we agree on some steps to move in that general direction?

CHAPTER 5

Where to Handle Disagreements

The biggest fear when establishing a leader in the family is that this person could stifle feedback or steamroll others. How can we make sure there is room for healthy pushback while still maintaining a unified team? There are a lot of books that talk about how to disagree, but I think you should first agree about *where* to disagree.

In startups, the ideal dynamic for disagreements is to be *unified in public* and eager to *disagree in private*.

Unified in Public

Presenting a unified front to your team, the public, clients, and so on is the best practice in all organizations, not just startups. There are three big benefits to this:

1. **Unity reinforces leadership authority.** As a group of leaders, you must reinforce each other's authority wherever possible.

Contradicting your colleagues in front of the team undermines someone's credibility—yours, theirs, or both. It also allows others to challenge governance, which can be massively unproductive.

2. **Unity demonstrates healthy conflict resolution.** If you can present a unified front internally and externally, you have a healthy team that resolves inevitable conflicts. It demonstrates maturity and trustworthiness, two essential ingredients for healthy partnerships and teams.
3. **Unity protects consistency in messaging.** As we discussed in the previous chapter, a major responsibility of an organization's leaders is to drive organizational clarity. Contradictions only muddy the waters for the team.

I clearly remember learning this lesson from my boss, Jim, in my early twenties while working for a young startup. Jim was an incredible leader. Even though I was twenty-four, he gave me immense responsibility, genuinely asked for my opinion, and invited me into high-stakes meetings with seasoned executives. One day, we were meeting with some high-profile C-suite executives of Fortune 100 companies.

At one point, an executive asked a question, and Jim gave an answer that I thought was incorrect. I piped up, "Actually, Jim, the number is x," and I explained the reason why. He thanked me for the clarification (it was kind of a minor point) and continued the original conversation. I figured I'd been helpful, and it didn't seem like a big deal.

Afterward, Jim asked me to chat in his office. It was common for us to debrief and discuss next steps after a big meeting. He asked me to close the door, and then he got kind of red and spoke sternly to me: "Listen to me, Blake. *Never* contradict your commanding officer in public. EVER. Behind closed doors, you can say whatever you want to me, and I will listen. But *never* contradict me like that again. Do you understand?" It was the only time I ever saw Jim get angry.

At the time, I thought he was showing that he cared more about "getting the sale" than he did about the truth. The number I said was correct; he was wrong. What I didn't realize then was I had weakened our team in front of a group of major clients. There was something even more important than the numbers in that conversation: The client was assessing what type of team we were and whether we could be trusted.

Years later, it makes me laugh to think about a twenty-four-year-old in a room full of fifty-something business titans saying, "Actually . . ." about some number I can't even remember now. But I did learn a lifelong lesson that day: A crack in a unified front will be much more memorable than whatever caused the crack.

The same is true in parenting. Contradicting your spouse in front of your children weakens their authority. Arguing with your kid or spouse in front of their friends demeans them. Maintaining a unified front reinforces that you are both on each other's team. But where *can* you disagree?

Radical Candor

In private, all bets should be off when it comes to disagreement. The term for this idea is *radical candor*, and it comes from the eponymous book by Kim Scott.[1] Scott explains that behind closed doors, great teams are not afraid to care deeply and challenge one another directly. She argues that for the good of the team as a whole, we should not let bad behavior or poor thinking continue just because it's "nice." Avoiding confrontation when we see bad behavior or poor thinking is highly selfish because we're putting our desire for approval above the well-being of the other person and the team.

Is radical candor good for a family? Well, before you light up your spouse or kids, let's talk through the process.

1. **Care personally.** To practice radical candor, you have to be deeply connected to the people on your team as individuals, not just workers.
2. **Challenge directly.** Assuming point #1 is in place, you should feel free to confront issues head-on without sugarcoating them, for the good of both the person and the organization.
3. **Encourage feedback.** As a leader, you should not only give feedback but also create a safe space and regularly request other people's honest opinions about your work and behavior.
4. **Gauge delivery.** Effective confrontation delivery is a developed skill. You will have to regularly assess your tone to make sure it's not muddying the message. You can be too aggressive or too passive, and it will take practice to find the right balance. Pro tip: Habits rooted in masculine energy (routines, systems, mastery) often improve with clear correction. Habits rooted in feminine energy (nurturing, aesthetics, hospitality) often flourish with clear affirmation.
5. **Act on the feedback.** Feedback should always lead to action. To create a culture of radical candor, your team needs to see that their input actually makes a difference.
6. **Foster an environment of openness.** Going beyond an interpersonal dynamic, you have to create a culture across your team that encourages everyone to communicate with radical candor. One of the best illustrations of this process is in *Start-Up Nation*, a book that chronicles why the nation of Israel is so overrepresented in the tech world. Authors Dan Senor and Saul Singer talk about the culture of the Israeli Defense Force and how the urgency they feel by being surrounded by their enemies results in a culture of "the best idea wins." The authors describe Israel's culture as one of "insatiable questioning of authority" and "determined informality," which contributes to its innovative environment.[2]

If we want the best thinking and culture, we must be open to giving and receiving criticism internally.

How Does This Work at Home?

All right, let's talk about the household. Take a moment right now to be honest with yourself about your marriage. On a scale of 1 to 10, how do you score on having a unified front? How do you score on radical candor?

Team Rating

	Spouse #1		Spouse #2	
	I score myself	*I score my spouse*	*I score myself*	*I score my spouse*
Radical Candor				
Unified Front				

Most people tend to lean more one way than the other, but what you need is balance. Here are a few follow-up questions for you and your partner to discuss:

- Why did you put that number?
- Can you give me a specific example that illustrates an area of strength or weakness?
- What's one thing I could change to raise my score in your eyes?

Now *that's* a conversation!

Tips for Increasing Radical Candor

If you both rated yourselves low in radical candor, here are some ways to get better at embracing conflict:

1. **Schedule structured feedback time.** Chandler and I have weekly, quarterly, and annual appointments for discussing any issues in our lives. Our meetings naturally surface things that could lead to criticism or a need to change. By putting it on the calendar, we create dedicated space to address these things rather than hoping we'll get up the courage in the middle of a busy day. (Note: Do NOT do this during date night. It will ruin it.)
2. **Trust each other's intentions.** I once heard this phrase: "We never question each other's intentions, but we always question each other's judgment." Recognizing the difference is huge. When Chandler challenges me, I know she does not think I want to harm anyone or anything; she just disagrees with my judgment. The truth is, we all need people to question our judgment. The best results always come from many counselors challenging our assumptions.
3. **Learn to listen well.** People are rarely good listeners; we tend to spend our time planning what to say next. Simple things like validating the other person's feelings, rearticulating what they're saying without judgment, and reorienting to the safety of the relationship will do wonders in helping you lean in to conflict when it happens.
4. **Don't be scared of conflict.** Respectful feedback in relationships is healthy. As parents, we owe it to our families to nip our own bad behavior or thinking in the bud before it grows and hurts someone. By getting around people who do conflict well and by observing others who don't, Chandler and I have grown in our belief that without healthy conflict, our marriage and family would suffer.

Tips for Increasing Your Unified Front

What if you're already *really* comfortable with radical candor but need to work on having a more unified front?

1. **Get on the same page.** Often, a lack of unification is the fruit of a root problem: a lack of clarity. Do the hard work (behind closed doors) to establish a mutually shared mission, vision, values, and goals. We will look at these factors in more detail throughout the book.
2. **Present a united decision.** Once you make a decision—even if you disagree and decide to commit anyway—accept and embrace it. For example, if you wanted to do something on the social calendar and the other person didn't, don't say, "I wanted to, but my spouse said no." Instead, just say, "We're not going to be able to make it." This shows respect and solidarity with your partner, and it will build you both up.
3. **Support each other publicly.** Even if you disagree or hear something inaccurate, wait until you're in private to correct or push back on your spouse. It's not that they can't handle it. It's just that the world is *teeming* with people willing and able to shut you down or correct you, while only a few have your back. Show up for each other this way.
4. **Resolve conflicts internally.** Keep your disagreements between the two of you. Don't dish to your friends and *definitely* don't dish to your kids. "Getting a third opinion" or just "venting" to an acquaintance will weaken your bond, so don't do it. If you get to a place where you need actual assistance, bring in a professional counselor or trusted adviser to help you both.

Being a unified parenting team that can be honest with each other is essential for cultivating a healthy culture within your family. The time you spend on this will have a *massive* effect on your marriage and family as a whole.

> Getting "good" at communicating is hard. It's easy to take offense, and it's easy to speak without forethought. As you're both growing in your communication skills, give your partner grace as they mature. You don't do this perfectly, and neither do they. When you feel offense rising up in you during a difficult conversation, remember this person is on your team. They love you and want what is best for you, even when that means sharing an uncomfortable truth. Give your spouse the grace to give you feedback imperfectly. Give yourself the grace to hear the love in that feedback, even when it stings.

ACTION PLAN

I think you know what you need to do, but here are the steps:

- Grab some time with your spouse and go through the rating questions for radical candor and having a united front.
- Answer these questions together:
  - Why did you put that number?
  - Can you give me a specific example that illustrates an area of strength or weakness?
  - What's one thing I could change to raise my score in your eyes?

CHAPTER 6

How to Handle Disagreements

If you have two human beings, you will eventually have disagreements. This is normal and unavoidable. What makes other persons enjoyable and interesting is that they are *not* us, which means they have different desires, thoughts, and opinions.

In friendships, different points of view make for really fun debates and interesting conversations. The problem is that when we are teammates with someone, whether in business or in raising a family, our differences directly influence each other. If we are not aligned with our team, we will instinctively feel threatened. So, how do we prepare for this and manage conflict when it happens?

Tips on Resolving Conflict Within the Family

I have typically saved tips for the end of the chapter, but due to the combustible nature of this topic, I'm going to start with them.

1. **Sometimes you need MORE conflict.** A relationship without conflict means either (a) there are not a lot of decisions being made or (b) bad decisions are being made. If you are in this

kind of relationship, make sure to have regularly scheduled time to discuss issues in your lives. These discussions likely won't turn into dynamic fights like in some other relationships, but they will lead to better decision-making. Many relationships benefit from more conflict, not less.

2. **Sometimes you need LESS conflict.** Are you prone to having a lot of fights? This is a sign of relational immaturity, and it is going to hurt your ability to succeed within any organization. Work on this. Read books, go to counseling, and uncover the underlying issues that drive your need for conflict.
3. **Sleep on it.** When my wife and I got married, someone told us to "never let the sun set on your anger"—meaning don't go to bed mid-argument. We followed this rule for years, and some of our worst dynamics happened late at night. Eventually, we realized we were not very good at navigating conflict when we were both tired. I do think there is wisdom in seeking to resolve conflict quickly (our rule is within twenty-four hours). But sometimes, if you just get some sleep, the issue naturally disappears. If I find myself bothered by something at or after 10 p.m. now, I tend to tell my wife that I love her and I'm going to sleep. We even have a name for when everything starts to look dismal: "sad o'clock." And 90 percent of the time, I wake up the next morning with no issue.
4. **Overlooking an offense is strength.** When we were kids on the playground, many of us learned to survive by "not taking it" from anyone. If someone insults you, you have to have a quick comeback or prove yourself superior in some way. This is, by definition, childish. King Solomon, the wisest man ever to live, wrote that it is a person's "glory to overlook an offense" (Prov. 19:11). In general, your path of growth should be toward becoming unoffendable. If you are just as or even more offendable this year as you were five years ago,

it means you are not growing, and you need to look into this and fix it.

5. **Get professional counseling.** If you have tried a couple of rounds of working through deep relational confrontation and can't make progress, get professional counseling. If you want to protect and reinforce your family against potential harm, get professional counseling. This is a common practice among business cofounders for a reason: It works. This relationship is too important to keep going in disharmony, so find a counselor, get to the root of the issues, develop the necessary skills, and start playing offense with the world and your vision for it.

Types of Conflict

Now that we have the tips out of the way, let's talk through the four different types of conflict we see within teams.

1. **Intellectual conflict** is the most basic type of conflict with another person. You disagree about how to categorize something, what its implications are, or how it should be addressed. Do the dishes with another person, and you will find an intellectual conflict: Do the bowls go on the top or bottom shelf? At work, this type of conflict translates into "I like this design more than that one."
2. **Relational conflict** arises from minor differences in personality, communication, values, style, or trust. Spend enough time with any group, and you'll encounter relational conflicts such as, "When you made that joke, it offended me," or "Why didn't you tell me about that meeting?"
3. **Shallow conflict** is often unintentional, unconscious, not deeply considered, or low-stakes conflict. A shallow conflict might be something like disagreeing on what color a logo

should be or a slip of the tongue that you didn't realize hurt someone's feelings. You can work these things out pretty routinely and quickly as long as both people act in good faith.

4. **Deep conflict** involves an issue that is tied deeply to someone's values, identity, or intention, and it hits a lot harder. These are fundamental differences in core personality, values, communication style, vision of a good life, overall strategic direction, and so forth. Both parties have deeply considered their "side" and are unlikely to move on the issue. A deep conflict might be a disagreement about something like vision, workplace culture, strategy, or fundamental values.

Putting everything together, we get these four quadrants:

The Conflict Chart

	Intellectual	**Relational**
Shallow	Squabble	Snag
Deep	Schism	Rift

Shallow Intellectual Disagreement: Squabble

When you have a shallow intellectual conflict—a squabble—the most important thing to do upfront is determine who will be the ultimate decision-maker on this issue. This places the correct person in the "judge" seat, where they become less of a persuader and more of a listener. The judge's job is to listen to all sides, take them into account, and make a decision.

For instance, if I don't like the color of the logo my creative director put together, I can start out by saying, "To be clear, this is *your* decision. I just want to share my concerns with what I'm seeing." If we have a healthy working relationship, this should put the creative director at ease, remind them they are in control, and encourage them to be curious about my perspective without feeling threatened.

On the flip side, if I'm working with a freelancer, I can clarify that I'm the decision-maker by saying, "In order for me to be comfortable going forward with this design, I need to see a couple more options for x, y, and z."

Most squabbles that become a "big deal" typically happen because there is ambiguity about who the ultimate decision-maker is. If you discover that a decision doesn't have an owner, solve that issue first.

In the family, if two kids are fighting over a toy, a great question to ask is, "Whose toy is this?" By establishing an owner, you can then work through character issues like sharing, generosity, and being considerate—all within the context of having a clear decision-maker.

Shallow Relational Conflict: Snag

Snags are inevitable. As long as you are with other people, they will hurt your feelings. My rule of thumb is the person who got "snagged" should be the one to bring up the issue. I actually tell people this when we become friends: "My assumption is that you and I are good. If we're not, I need *you* to tell me." And as my older kids are becoming teenagers, I regularly warn them, "I know I'm going to say something stupid at some point that hurts your feelings. I *need* you to tell me when I do that."

The reason I make these statements is because I'm overly sensitive to other people's emotional states, and I often perceive criticism or problems that are not really there. Clarifying the solution upfront helps me avoid overthinking about interactions. It also prevents passive aggressive behavior by shifting the responsibility to the individual(s) affected.

When I snag someone, I follow these steps:

1. **I apologize.** Once I understand how I have hurt someone, I apologize and explain my intentions. "I'm sorry for embarrassing you. My intention was to do x, but I see how that hurt you." (Both sides typically have some blame to share, so you can take turns here.) Resist the temptation to be 100 percent right, especially with teens. You likely *could* have done something differently, and you need to model how to humbly apologize.
2. **I reinforce.** Next, I typically helicopter up and reinforce the strength and meaning of our relationship. "I love spending time with you, and I admire your hard work in your school." Again, it is important for both parties to build up the other person.
3. **I commit to change.** The final thing I do is reassure them that I'll try harder in the future to be sensitive to this vulnerability. "In the future I'll try to be less flippant when I give feedback." I also ask if there is anything else we need to talk about while we're here.

On the flip side, sometimes *you* are the one who gets snagged. Someone says or does something, and you can't seem to let it go. Here is my process when I get snagged:

1. **I try to drop it.** I ask myself questions like, *Will this bother me in a year?* or *Was this person's intention to hurt my feelings?* Sometimes I can drop it, and other times I can't. If I can't, I move to step 2.
2. **I use the "magic phrase."** Someone once told me the way to solve any problem is to use this magic phrase: "I want things to be good between you and me." If two people can both say this in good faith, then without exception there *will* be restoration. So, if I can't drop something, I come to the person and say something like, "Hey, I'm feeling off from a

conversation we had earlier. I really want things to be good between us, so can we talk?" Reassuring the person of your desire for reconciliation, especially with teens, will help them feel less defensive and more open to making things right.

3. **"I felt x when you did y."** Phrasing here is extremely important. As long as you both use this framework, you can quickly get to whatever the snag was. If you're the one bringing it up, you can start with something like, "I felt really angry when you shut me down in that meeting."

I make sure to listen carefully to the other person's perspective and acknowledge their intent, which often helps clarify misunderstandings. Once the issue is resolved, I let it go. Whether you snag someone or are snagged yourself, the goal is the same: to restore the relationship and move forward with greater trust and understanding.

Deep Intellectual Disagreement: Schism

A deep intellectual disagreement is a schism and should only occur when the decision is so important or broadly impactful that it requires mutual agreement (e.g., where to live).

The key here is research. Whoever calls the meeting to discuss the direction on this decision holds the responsibility to show up with background information, context, potential solutions, and a well-researched recommendation. Put it in writing.

Once it's time for the meeting, there should be no discussion until everyone present has read and marked up the document. From there you're now ready for a vigorous debate because everyone should have the same amount of information.

This is the process that almost all levels of Amazon employees follow when making big decisions. The person presenting the decision/calling the meeting does the most work and then starts the meeting with thirty minutes or so of quiet "study time" for the rest of the team members present.[1]

As long as everyone is mutually committed to what's best for the team, this process will likely produce the best outcome. I remember as a twelve-year-old, I put together a presentation for my parents on getting a trampoline, outlining safety concerns and how to mitigate them. It showed my parents how serious I was, and they gave the idea much more thought because of that.

Deep Relational Conflict: Rift

A deep relational conflict—a rift—is, in my experience, the most dangerous relational threat. The problem is that if a rift goes on long enough, you stop seeing the other person as a human being, and they become an imaginary version you use to reinforce your point of view. This is the primary reason marriages end and children become estranged. We have to learn how to heal rifts.

This concept comes from a great book called *Leadership and Self-Deception* by the Arbinger Institute. Where there is deep relational hurt, you put the other person in a "box" where they are no longer whole human beings, and instead you see them as a threat or obstacle. Their needs are less important than your needs, and you unconsciously resist whatever the other person wants, even when they are acting in good faith. Unless you get "out of the box," the relationship is likely doomed.[2]

If you realize you are in a rift with your partner or child, you must make the effort to reconnect. The way to do this is to get curious about what *they* are (or have been) experiencing. Here is a quick outline you can go through together:

1. Try to see the situation from an outside or third perspective by asking, "How would someone else describe what has happened between us?"

2. Tell your person, "I have some thoughts on why this is the case, but first I'd like to hear your thoughts."
3. Listen and repeat back to show you have heard their point of view. Ask yourself if you truly understand it. If not, ask more questions.
4. Share your point of view.
5. Work together to build a united story and mutual commitment going forward.

I grew up in the conservative Christian culture of the 1990s. I don't know if it was ever explicitly said in church or in our home, but the message I internalized was clear: A godly "helper" was someone who followed her husband's lead in everything. (FYI, a more accurate translation of the Hebrew word used here might be "helper against"—not in the sense of opposition, but as a strong, equal counterpart.)

When I fell in love with Blake, I fell hard. He was (and still is) everything I ever wanted in a husband: funny, handsome, smart, raised similarly to me, driven, and ambitious. And he wanted a big family. It felt like the perfect match.

When we got married, I brought all of my 1990s ideas about biblical womanhood into our relationship. I loved God. I loved my husband. And I was determined to be the best "helper" I could be.

So I agreed with him—on pretty much everything. I tried not to have too many opinions. If Blake had an idea, I was always supportive. I didn't trust my own intuition, and I didn't believe it was okay to share it. I thought I was being a "good" wife—someone who supported her husband, no matter what.

After a while, Blake began to notice that I rarely had a differing opinion and, when he asked for my thoughts on something, I usually didn't have much to say. One day, he sat down with me and said, "Hey, I NEED you to push back on me. I really value your opinion. I need your discernment. I need your help in leading this family—and that help looks like you telling me when I'm wrong, even if I don't see it."

He didn't realize it at the time, but he was confronting a deeply warped view I had of womanhood. He wasn't just giving me permission to use my voice, he was begging me to bring all of the wisdom and strength God had given me into our marriage. He didn't want a yes-woman. He wanted a partner.

With that new understanding, we actually began to have more conflict—but it was healthy conflict. We learned how to communicate and work through our disagreements instead of avoiding them. We experienced deeper intimacy because we were finally bringing our full selves into the relationship.

Blake's invitation for me to lean against him gave our marriage the traction to pursue the things God had placed in front of us. Together.

ACTION PLAN

Your relationships with your family members are obviously much deeper and more enmeshed than those with work colleagues, and the stakes of getting this right are significantly higher. So I recommend pulling out the conflict chart when you have a conflict with your spouse or child and using it as a tool to help you work through what's going on.

- **Locate.** Together, look at the chart and point to what you think this argument is. You'll notice that as soon as you do this, some of the "heat" goes out of it.
- **Prioritize.** Sometimes, you'll realize that you are in different places—you may be arguing something relational while the other person is arguing something intellectual. My rule of thumb is to start with the relational hurt *first* and then move to the intellectual argument. Our brains are wired to have our relational dynamics trump our intellectual dynamics, and you won't be able to make a clear intellectual decision until the relationship is shored up.

AREA 2

DIRECTION

Almost nothing is more important for any organization than knowing why it exists, what it cares about, and where it is going. Groups without direction meander reactively and opportunistically through time and eventually falter. Groups with direction proactively create a reality in which they thrive. And this is also true of the family.

In terms of effectiveness, organizations that are clearly purpose-driven grow three times faster on average than those that are not.[1] Leaders ignore this at their own risk—I don't know of *any* other tool that on average delivers 300 percent more effectiveness. Purpose really matters!

Also, people LOVE working on a team with a purpose:

> Purpose-oriented companies have higher productivity and growth rates, along with a more satisfied workforce who stay longer with them. Our research shows that such companies report 30 percent higher levels of workforce retention than their competitors.[2]

It makes sense, right? When you're working, you want to know that what you're doing adds up to something bigger than just your contribution. We'd all like to know that our efforts have some level of significance in the world or in the lives of others.

Why would family be any different? In his exploration of human motivation, Viktor Frankl famously identified meaning as the pinnacle of human needs. If we want to create a deep, lasting bond with our family, we do need connection, but even more, we need a meaningful direction to pursue together.

Given this, why do some organizations still trudge along without a clear direction? Here are three questions I've noticed myself and others asking that tend to keep us from setting a clear purpose:

1. **What if things change?** The tricky part of proactively setting a trajectory for a family or business is that reality often disrupts our plans. I love this quote from legendary boxer Mike Tyson: "Everyone has plans until they get hit for the first time."[3] So is it even worth setting a plan? Why not just roll with the punches? Because teams need clarity—especially in the midst of change. Companies need a purpose as their "true north," even if they never hit it exactly. And families, especially, are constantly changing as younger members physically and emotionally transform every year or two. That's why we need *more* direction, not less.
2. **What if my team thinks I'm lame?** As the leader tasked with setting the vision, I often felt like it was cheesy to stand in front of my team and talk about our big mission. It's a vulnerable act to stand in front of a group of people and say, "This is where we're going, and this is why it's important." It takes courage to share an aspirational vision with the critical eye of a teen child or reluctant team member. Part of being a leader is pushing through that embarrassment and doing the awkward thing because you know it's better for everyone.

3. **Isn't there more important work to be done?** Even though we know that clarifying our purpose guarantees an average of 300 percent greater effectiveness, it won't solve any problems *today*. In fact, it might make the urgent problems of today worse because we took time to solve the big picture. There is laundry to be done, a yard to be mowed, and children to be driven all over town—and we're going to spend time working on our *vision*? A core requirement of every leader is to balance the urgency of today with the most important work for the organization's future. If we don't, we'll live in the tyranny of the urgent and never create a future where we thrive.

I'm sure in your own life you can remember the best teams that you've been a part of; they were teams where the mission was something larger than just yourself. Maybe it was an athletic club, a volunteer group, a band or orchestra, or a work cohort. There is something really special that happens when we submit our personal desires for the greater good and act as a unit.

> I'm a "don't think about it too long—just attack the problem" kind of person, so the process of laying out our family mission, vision, and values originally felt like we were becoming *less* productive. But taking the time to clarify and refine our direction has helped us make decisions so much more easily. The result has felt like finally taking the training wheels off and really zooming ahead. It's foundational work that will bring your entire family onto the same page. So, in this next section, we're going to walk through the core components of creating a family with purpose. My hope is that you come away with a clear picture and added momentum in the direction you all want to go.

CHAPTER 7

Define Your Family Values

Let's talk about values, but first a little context: Corporations in the early 1900s were mainly focused on profit and growth. After World War II, a handful of companies (like HP and IBM) started focusing a bit more on their corporate culture, and they began to see significant growth compared to their peers. This shift led to a massive emphasis on corporate culture in the 1980s, and now it's common in companies everywhere.

An organization's "values" are typically five to ten defining character traits or aspirations its leaders will use for making major decisions and shaping its culture. One of my favorite examples is Nike's values that Phil Knight wrote in 1980:

1. Our business is change.
2. We're on offense. All the time.
3. Perfect results count—not a perfect process.
   Break the rules: fight the law.
4. This is as much about battle as about business.
5. Assume nothing.
   Make sure people keep their promises.
   Push yourselves push others.
   Stretch the possible.

6. Live off the land.
7. Your job isn't done until the job is done.
8. Dangers
   Bureaucracy
   Personal ambition
   Energy takers vs. energy givers
   Knowing our weaknesses
   Don't get too many things on the platter
9. It won't be pretty.
10. If we do the right things we'll make money d—n near automatic.[1]

Okay, so how is this relevant to family life? I know concepts like "battle," "offense," and "break the rules" might not be what your three-year-old needs at this point in their life, but bear with me. What are some potential benefits of posting your values like this?

1. **Values create a culture.** What I love about values is that you can *feel* what the company is like in the words. You can get a sense of whether this organization is going to be a good fit for you.
2. **Values influence future strategies.** Saying something like "We're on offense. All the time," means if anyone in a strategy meeting tries to suggest a defensive maneuver, others can point to the wall and say, "That's not what we do here." It locks in something deeper than strategy.
3. **Values tell you who NOT to be.** I love Nike's list of "dangers"—Phil Knight clearly articulates what he *doesn't* want the company to be.
4. **Values pre-answer questions.** If someone at Nike wanted to pitch a big, expensive project, they knew the first thing they'd hear back would be "Live off the land." That means rather than spending time to develop the plan, make the

recommendation, and get the feedback, they could refer to the values and already know that a costly idea won't get approved.

5. **Values set the bar.** When you say, "Perfect results count—not a perfect process," it sets a bar to do whatever it takes to get those perfect results. Setting a high bar is a huge part of being a leader, and if you can point to it in writing—in a founding document like this—then it feels even more real.

Above everything else, values are a core element of your job as a leader to drive clarity. It's almost a cliché in business now because literally every company does it, but they do it for a reason. Ignore it at your own peril.

Creating Your Family Values

Let's talk about how this fits into your family life. I've found creating a list of family values to be incredibly helpful in setting the culture of our family. We review one value a week during family dinner, and we talk about stories or examples that resonate with that value. I've discovered the more we talk about our values, the more our kids really internalize them.

Here are some writing exercises to go through with your spouse (or your spouse and kids). At the end, you will combine the prompts into a list of family values. Don't try to write and edit at the same time. You have the rest of your life to add, subtract, and change things, so just start with what feels right now and don't overthink it.

Prompt 1: When you think about the people you admire in your life, what attributes make them stand out to you?

Encourage your entire family to list the people they admire and then write down descriptors or phrases that capture them.

Example: My friend Christopher

- Curious: Has SO many interests; he's curious about everything.
- Bold: He's willing to call out good things in other people when he sees them and challenge things that he thinks are off.
- Present: I appreciate that when he's in a conversation he's not looking around for the next conversation—he's fully present.
- Playful: I like that he doesn't take anything too seriously and will often make jokes.

Prompt 2: Name four or five historical or fictional characters you admire. What traits do they have?

This is a similar exercise to prompt 1 but for characters from books, movies, or history. Here's an example from Chandler:

Example: Joan of Arc

- Courage: She was willing to put her life on the line for something greater than herself.
- Persistence: She didn't get discouraged and quit early in this life—she kept going.
- Honesty: She held true to her beliefs, even when it would have been easier to deny her visions.

Prompt 3: What angers you more than most people?

This is kind of a funny prompt, but it's amazing what it reveals about your values. Chandler and I wrote:

- People acting helpless when they could do something for themselves.
- When people take themselves too seriously.
- When grown men use baby talk.

- When there is a new person in the room and no one greets them or includes them.

Prompt 4: Hold off the critic.

Share what you've written as a family. This is a time to listen and reflect without judgment. Any creative process requires us to mute our inner (or outer) critic while we create. Some people have the gift of critical thinking, but all critique needs to be held back until the ideas have been fully fleshed out. I like to think of it as a flowering shrub: Pruning is really important, but not at the sprout stage. If you criticize your children's or spouse's ideas too early, they will believe you don't value their opinion.

> When giving feedback to your spouse or children, consider using the design framework of "I like. I wish. I wonder." First, list what you like about what they wrote. Then specifically explain what you wish was different. Finally, you can share ideas you are wondering about that were prompted by their suggestion. I've found this is far more collaborative than just jumping into correcting a creative work.

Prompt 5: Put it all together.

Now you have random lists of things your entire family admires and things that drive you all crazy. Start to gather them together into a core list of attributes or concepts. What themes emerge? What feels like it's missing?

Now the fun part: Keep-Kill-Combine, which comes from a great book, *Traction*, by Gino Wickman.[2]

- **Keep.** Give every person three votes. If you could each only keep three items, which three would you keep? Cast your votes separately. (Hopefully there will be one or two things that overlap during "Combine.")

- **Kill.** If you each had to kill two items on the list, which two would you kill? Why? (The "Keep" list is off-limits.)
- **Combine.** Go through the remaining list and combine anything that naturally has overlap. For example, if Chandler had "lightheartedness" and I had "playfulness," we could combine them into one concept: "playfulness/lightheartedness."

Prompt 6: Make it more than a word.

After you narrow down your list of values, try to go beyond a single word for each one and follow up with a sentence or two explaining it. Best practice is to then list examples that go with each value as well. A single word can't embody a value nearly enough and leaves way too much open for interpretation.

And there you have it: an initial draft of your family values! Your next step is to display your list in your home. Make posters. Your kids could draw pictures for each value or use Canva or some other design software. We have some friends who paid a designer to make beautifully illustrated pictures for each of their values, and I can still name their values from memory from being in their home.

How to Use Your Family Values

You might be thinking, *Great, now how do I use these things?* Here are some ideas:

- **Make big decisions.** When you have big decisions going forward, look at your list of values. Ask yourselves, *If we were to live out our values in this decision, what would we do? What would a person who embodies these values do?*
- **Have a "values dinner."** Once a week, we'll pick one of our values and talk about it as a family. I'll introduce the word, explain what it means, and share some examples

from movies or books that illustrate it. Then I'll ask if anyone has examples in their life of people embodying that value. Over time, as you repeat them, the kids (and you and your spouse) will start to adopt these words as common language.

- **Look at conflict.** If you find yourself in a conflict with someone—outside or within the family—pay attention and ask yourself, *Is this violating one of our values?* Often, the really difficult conflicts stem from a values issue.
- **Examine your week.** Thinking about your week, how much of it reflects your values? If you value something like "creativity" but your family never does anything art- or music-related in your average week, maybe something needs to change. A good life is one that is consistent with what you value.
- **Check in on your kids.** Chandler and I have started evaluating our kids (without them present) according to our values. We've found this gives us language when we feel like something is off; it's often because they aren't living up to our family values as much as they could. This process can set the stage for intentional training, meaningful conversations, and exercises to go deeper.
- **Expand the list with your older children.** Over time, you may realize that your teen or adult child is embodying a *new* value for your family. What a beautiful thing to communicate their individual value by adding it to your family values and begin growing as a family in that direction.
- **Develop "values sermons."** Over time, it will help to have your own "TED Talk" on hand for each value—something you can use to reenergize everyone (especially your kids) around a specific value. This might include certain phrases you repeat and stories you tell. Again, this aligns with one

of the primary jobs of a leader: to constantly champion and reinforce the organizational clarity you create.

Updating Your Family Values

Over time, you'll want to rewrite and revise your family values list. We try to schedule our edits no more often than during each quarterly meeting, but we have definitely found the updates to be helpful as our family finds its unique values and voice.

> After years of crafting and trying to live out our values, there's nothing sweeter than seeing our kids reflect those values back to us. It's reflected in the characters they resonate with in books and movies and the kinds of friends they seek out. They have been deeply shaped by our values, and now it's just become a part of who they are.

ACTION PLAN

I know—that was a lot! The best thing you can do is find some time with your older family members or just your spouse to go through the steps.

- **Define your values.** Work together to create a list of core family values using the prompts.
- **Refine the list.** Use Keep-Kill-Combine to narrow down your values, then go beyond one word by adding a sentence of definition or examples for each value.
- **Integrate the values into your family life.** Use them to guide big decisions and reflect on conflicts, and discuss one value weekly at dinner.

CHAPTER 8

Craft Your Family Mission

A mission is a concise statement of why your organization exists. It needs to be short and snappy enough that everyone in the organization can recite it from memory. Some great examples from famous companies include:

- "To organize the world's information and make it universally accessible and useful."—Google
- "To revolutionize space technology, with the ultimate goal of enabling people to live on other planets."—SpaceX
- "We're in the business to save our home planet."—Patagonia
- "To bring inspiration and innovation to every athlete in the world."—Nike
- "To save people money so they can live better."—Walmart

A great mission statement has the following attributes:

- **It's BIG.** A mission is typically the boldest of the big-picture tools. It makes the picture so big you could dedicate a lifetime to it.

- **It's inspiring.** You'll notice that the companies listed above are all for-profit businesses, but none of them have the mission of "make a profit"—because that is not inspiring. It puts profit into the category of "fuel" to achieve its grander, human-centric mission. Similarly, in family, your goal has to go beyond survival—it has to transcend to something elevating.
- **It's meaningful.** As humans, we want to be part of something that we think has lasting meaning. Whether it's saving the planet, helping others, or advancing a cause, tying your organization to something with lasting meaning will ignite a passion that simple goals just can't accomplish.
- **It's memorable.** This is key. A mission statement requires some copywriting. Vision can ramble a bit. Values get follow-up examples and sentences. But a mission needs to be as much a catchphrase as it is a statement of direction.

So, how can you apply this thinking to your family life? Is this even a good idea for families?

In the best organizations, a mission statement gives people a deep sense of purpose—the fuel of inspiration that helps them do their best work, such as world-changing innovation. Research tells us that having a sense of purpose is one of the necessary ingredients for staving off depression in life.[1] A life with a bigger mission is exciting; without it, existence can become tired and repetitive.

Why not do a creative act of service for those in your care who can benefit from the inspiration of being part of a mission bigger than what anyone can realistically do in this lifetime? For our family, having a mission has given us

- a "why" to lean on during hard times,
- a "true north" to guide us when we get overwhelmed, and
- a "rallying cry" to unite us when we naturally focus on our own needs.

Who knows—maybe writing a family mission statement could even be a little fun?

Crafting Your Family Mission Statement

First of all, you could take inspiration from corporate life and plan this as a day away—just you and your spouse. It's definitely worth getting away for this exercise, as there is something about being in a new environment that will help you approach these questions with a fresh perspective.

Like discovering your family values, this process starts with writing prompts. I suggest you write separately and then come back together to share and discuss.

Prompt 1: Write your obituary.

Whoa, things just got really dark. I'm not trying to be morbid, but nothing reveals the moral of the story quite like the end. Try writing your own obituary as you would like it to be written.

Start with "(Insert your name) passed away at age eighty." Then write what you want to have been true of your life. What was your life's work? How many kids and grandkids did you have? What were your passions? How did you treat others? Just keep writing—no need to edit.

Now describe the family you've left behind. What are they known for? How do they affect the community in which they live? This can start to feel pretty emotional, but lean in to it and keep writing. When you're done, come back together with your spouse to share.

- Are there any noticeable themes?
- What surprised you about what you wrote?
- What surprised you about what your spouse wrote?
- Where are you on track for achieving this picture?

- What in your life do you feel needs to change to live up to this picture?

Prompt 2: List the movies, books, and historical organizations or families that inspire you.

What stirs your soul? Maybe make a list of your top ten most inspiring or moving films. What are their major themes? Here are some examples from Chandler's and my lists of movies (please don't judge us):

- *Dead Poets Society*
- *Les Misérables* (with Hugh Jackman, not Liam Neeson)
- *About Time*
- *Captain Fantastic*
- *The Internet's Own Boy*
- *It's a Wonderful Life*

What are the common themes across these movies that move us?

- **Perspective.** *Dead Poets Society* and *About Time* both have a way of helicoptering up beyond the day-to-day to what "the good life" is really all about.
- **Impact.** *The Internet's Own Boy* and *Les Misérables* both have elements of impacting the community or the world at large and "making a difference" culturally.
- **Home.** *It's a Wonderful Life*, *About Time*, and *Captain Fantastic* all have elements of home being the locus of where life happens (and specifically family being central to meaning).
- **People.** Without exception, each of these stories is about relationships. At the end of the day, I think connecting with other human beings is the most meaningful thing we can do in this world.

Prompt 3: Think bigger.

It's really easy for your mission to become a statement of values (e.g., "Be a family that is kind."). But that's not a mission—you just value kindness. The difference is that a mission has to do with *why* you exist, while a value has to do with *how* you will behave.

Prompt 4: Start listing mission statements until you cry.

Now that you have a picture of a meaningful end to your life and a list of attributes that really define meaning for you, it's time to draft your mission. I think the most helpful thing you can do is just start listing statements rapid-fire, one line at a time. Don't critique—just keep writing. As you do, pay attention to your feelings. Does something start to swell in you? If so, keep writing in that direction.

For example, I might start listing:

- Impact, family, home, people, perspective.
- To impact the world through family.
- To bring perspective and impact through our family.
- To be a home that brings perspective and impact.
- An impactful home.

Just keep writing until something pops. Chandler and I did this exercise and eventually came up with "Enter for refuge. Go out and restore."

Prompt 5: Include everyone.

Don't make your mission so narrow that your adult children will want nothing to do with it. If your children are young, how and if you really drive this mission home for them will affect if they *want* to be a part of it later. Make sure the mission is broad enough that they will still derive meaning from it as adults. For example, we could have made part of our mission "telling a better story" (because I'm a marketer and an entrepreneur), but what if one of our kids wants to be a doctor? You don't want to be so broad that it's meaningless, but you also don't want to be so narrow that it leaves out some members of your family.

A quick thought: Does your family of origin already have a mission, whether written or unwritten? Not every family has to invent their mission from scratch. It may be that your role is just to capture what's already been there for generations. Our friends Andrew and Rachel Peters found a newspaper article from the early 1900s that described how the Peters family helped start a town in rural Ohio. They both derived great meaning from this article and have used it to help shape the identity of their family today.

Review Your Mission Statement

I recently found our first mission statement, which we wrote in 2011. At the time it was so meaningful to me. Now it's nonsense. There's this complex diagram, and I honestly don't understand what I was trying to say. It's totally okay to make several iterations over the years. Your kids have new contributions. Life can bring new directions and passions. Your mission is a heading on a compass; you may take a winding path as you go, but it will become clearer the closer you get to the destination.

I want to end this chapter by saying I'm rooting for you and your family as you work on this together. This is an incredibly brave and creative act, and I think it will bless you, your marriage, and your family immensely if you create this clarity. May you go forth with courage and a servant's heart as you lead your family into a meaningful life.

> The exercises outlined in this chapter are so helpful at clarifying what's deeply important to your family. They're also pretty emotional. (I cried like a baby writing my own obituary.) This is work that gets to the very core of who you are and what you care about—it's deep! Set yourself

up for success by creating space in your day to rest and process those emotions, instead of just jumping from these exercises to the next task on your list.

ACTION PLAN

Get started on crafting your family mission with these quick steps:

- **Reflect on the end goal.** Write a brief vision of how you want to be remembered and what kind of legacy you'd like your family to leave.
- **List your inspirations.** Jot down movies, books, or themes that inspire you. Look for common themes that resonate with your family values.
- **Draft and refine.** Rapidly brainstorm simple mission statements. Keep writing until one of them feels deeply meaningful to you and your spouse.

CHAPTER 9

Cast a Vision for the Future

Your vision should be a description of a compelling and realistic future for your family in the next five to ten years. To help clarify, a mission describes *why* you do what you do, while a vision describes *what* you want to do or be in the future.

For example, as I shared in the previous chapter, this is our family mission statement: "Enter for refuge. Go out and restore."

Our family vision is the following:

- Build a 100,000-person audience for whom to create meaningful books, products, and e-courses, generating an ongoing revenue stream by 2027.
- Create opportunities (cofounding, employment, etc.) to work with our children by 2032.
- Live entirely on asset-based income by 2035, freeing up time to help with our children and grandchildren.
- Expand our home as a delightful destination, hosting space, and appropriate place for extended family and friends as we become the "hub" for the next generation (deck, dock, boat, expanded living room, etc.).

- Opportunistically buy the homes on our road for short-term rentals and extended family living.

The idea is to have a clear image of what a winning future looks like for your family. This is going to include finances, education, health, relationships, and fun.

Creating Your Family Vision

All right! Let's get to work creating your family vision. Similar to (or alongside) the development of your mission, I'd recommend getting away with your spouse (and perhaps older children). This will be work, but it can create a huge amount of clarity for your family.

Part 1: Write your vision ideas separately.

I recommend taking an hour for this. Go off on your own and write what you want to be true ten years from now for your family. I like using Mike Breen and Ben Sternke's "Five Capitals" as category prompts:

1. **Financial capital.** Financially, what do you want to be true for your family? What are your income streams? Savings goals? Spending strategies? (By the way, financial capital is not a goal in itself but rather the fuel for whatever goals you set.)
2. **Intellectual capital.** What do you want to be true intellectually/academically for each member of your family? Whether it's schools, books, accreditations, retreats, or something similar, what do you want to see happen for the further development of your minds?
3. **Physical capital.** What is the picture of your family's overall health ten years from now? What needs to be true to get there? Include diet, exercise, sleep, and so on in this.

4. **Relational capital.** What are the most important relationships in your life ten years from now? How will you invest in them to make sure they are strong?
5. **Spiritual capital.** If you are a person of faith, what does your relationship with God look like? If you are not, what is the most meaningful area of your life, and how will it have grown ten years from now?[1]

Write freely for each capital. Then go through and edit until each answer feels clear and concise.

> I know a lot of visually oriented people who will cut out pictures from magazines or use Pinterest to "envision" the future they want. I'm not personally wired this way, but I think the practice is a great idea. You can display it somewhere you see often to remind you where you are going. It's also a fun way to include kids and teens.

Part 2: Share and combine.

This part is fun. Take turns reading each portion out loud to your spouse, while the other person creates bullet points of the major elements. When you're both done, you should have a list of bullets for each of you. Combine any similar bullets and decide which items to keep or kill. For this exercise, try to be concise and only keep the bullets that deeply map to what you both want. If necessary, rank your notes and prioritize what is most important to you both.

Your vision doesn't have to incorporate all five capitals listed above, or only these five capitals. For example, Chandler and I exercise every day because it gives us energy and makes us feel happier. We don't have a vision for our physical health—we just know that the habit serves us.

Your vision should also have built-in trade-offs. It's fun to dream of a life where you travel for work and have dinner with your family every night, but it's not actually possible to do both at the same time! This is where your values will help inform your trade-off decisions. Your vision should say, "We're *not* going to do x so that we *can* do y."

There are few things more intimate than someone's desires and aspirations. Handle them with care. Sometimes we hold on to dreams for years without ever sharing them with anyone. Look to help your spouse clarify their aspirations *first* before criticizing or testing them for logic.

Part 3: Summarize.

Your goal is to summarize what you both are going after for your family: Trim all of this down to five sentences or less! For me, this is the hardest part. I've found it helpful to use AI here—I like to drop bullets into ChatGPT and ask for a summary. I'll end up editing that summary, but it gives me a good starting place.

That's it! Now you should have a clear vision to help drive clarity for your family.

Get in the habit of reviewing your family values, mission, and vision regularly and reciting them to each other until they become central to everything you do.

Can You Go Too Big?

In the past, Chandler and I set some really big visions and then failed to hit them. It's kind of discouraging and in some ways a waste of time. Try to set realistic visions that are a little closer to tactics and strategy than dreams.

There is nothing more empowering than accomplishing your vision early and asking, "Where should we go next?" But don't set your vision so low that it's no longer inspiring. If your vision feels inevitable or "more of the same," you may need to challenge yourself a little more. What *could* be possible? People tend to default too large or too small with vision—and those people often marry each other. I personally think this is a feature and not a bug.

How to Use Your Vision

Just having a statement of where you are going as a family will help you move forward in life with purpose. Often, the vision changes the closer you get to it. I've found that life with a big picture breeds more opportunities and results than life with no picture.

A vision is especially helpful when you have to make hard decisions. Rather than say, "We can't afford x vacation," you can frame it as, "We want y as a family. In order for us to do that, we have to say no to things like x." While it's possible to overuse this technique, it takes the negative points of denying your desires and puts them in the positive; you are moving toward embracing something you deeply want.

A team with a vision can get through pretty much anything, so congratulations on putting something so important in place. I hope it blesses your family immensely.

> Having a clear vision for what we want our life to look like has given us so much clarity. It's so much easier to make hard decisions when you have a clarified picture of the life for which you're making those hard decisions. Without that picture, you're bound to either passively stick with the status quo of what life serves you or erratically make one-off decisions that create chaos and instability for your people. The hard work of defining your vision individually and then as a couple and family will give momentum and stability to your family as you pursue it.

ACTION PLAN

I recommend creating your mission, vision, and values statements in the same season together, perhaps even on the same trip. As a review, here are the steps:

- Write your vision ideas separately, taking an hour to outline what you want for your family in ten years and using categories such as financial, intellectual, physical, relational, and spiritual goals.
- Share and combine your ideas, creating a consolidated bullet list of key elements and narrowing it down to what resonates most.
- Summarize your family vision into five sentences or less to clearly articulate where you're headed.
- Display and review your family's vision, mission, and values regularly to keep them central in daily life and guide big decisions.

CHAPTER 10

Set Meaningful Family Goals

Goals bridge the gap between the ethereal elements of the big picture— mission, vision, and values—and the reality of here and now. When we set goals, we start with our end vision and work our way back to our current state.

Typically, in an organization, leaders set annual goals at the beginning of the year, followed by quarterly goals that map to those annual goals. You can use this process to help your family too.

So, how do we set goals? Personally, I've always struggled with keeping my goals realistic. When I was running my company, I'd create an Excel spreadsheet with a projection of us tripling each year, assign each number to a person, and think, *My job here is done*. But then I'd start getting pushback from the team, asking, "How on earth are we supposed to do this?" This would frustrate me because as an optimist at some core level, I feel like if you believe you can do it, then you *can* do it. What I didn't know at the time was that I was treating goals like New Year's resolutions. They were wishful ideas, like "I'm going to lose twenty-five pounds," but had no plan, strategy, or trade-offs attached to them. They were just written desires.

What's interesting is that when you write your resolutions or desires, you actually get a small dopamine hit. As the author of the resolution, you feel like you're a little closer to your "goal" simply because you wrote it down—and it cost you nothing. In families, the most common goals I've seen (and written) have to do with college and retirement savings. It's great to write down the goal, but without a plan it's just like pinning a recipe on Pinterest with no intention of making it. It's vanity and, ultimately, a waste of time.

But then I learned about S.M.A.R.T. goals. I'm sure some of you have already heard of this, but for those who haven't, here's an introduction.

S.M.A.R.T. Goals

In 1981, George T. Doran, a journalist writing for *Management Review*, introduced the concept of making your objectives S.M.A.R.T. This acronym stands for:

- "**Specific**—target a specific area for improvement." Your goal needs to create a clear picture of what you will and will not do.
- "**Measurable**—quantify or at least suggest an indicator of progress." You should be able to tie your vision to a number you can measure in the future.
- "**Assignable**—specify who will do it." Your goal needs to be realistically achievable by a specific person. It's awesome to say, "We're going to be financially free," but you'd better back it up with a realistic plan that gives you at least 80 percent confidence you can achieve it.
- "**Realistic**—state what results can realistically be achieved, given available resources." Your goal needs to make sense with your values, mission, and vision. It would be weird if your family's goal was to buy multiple vacation homes

if your family mission and values are all about simplicity and contentment.

- "**Time-related**—specify when the result(s) can be achieved." The very best goals have a deadline written into them. By x date, you will either have accomplished the vision or not.[1]

How to Use S.M.A.R.T. Goals in Family Life

First of all, you need to get *specific*. As a continuation of the work you did for your vision, it's time to break down that big picture into specific parts. For example, one part of our family's financial vision in 2023 was "To have our day-to-day lives funded by passive income by 2027."

We then needed to think about *how* and *when*. At the time, we were about 35 percent funded by asset-based income, so the question was, "What would reasonable and meaningful progress look like toward this goal?" I thought reasonable progress would be 50 percent, so the goal I put under the financial capital header was this: "To have our day-to-day lives funded 50 percent by asset-based income in 2024."

The next step is to make the goal *measurable* and *assignable*. For us, this looked like:

- Through smart budgeting and doing yard/housework as a family, save $1,000 in our monthly budget by April 2024.
- Consistently live within our means/monthly budget for twelve months.
- Complete an e-course on optimizing short-term rentals by March 31 and implement all changes.

Do you see how this is starting to look a little more *real*? There are trade-offs, efforts, and initiatives that directly connect to this goal. The more a goal maps to tasks like this, the more likely you are to actually pull it off.

Watch Out

Easy, right? Unfortunately, probably not. There are some obstacles or errors likely coming your way.

1. **Forming overly optimistic goals.** This is my Achilles' heel. If I'm excited about a goal, I tend to think I can do it no matter what. The problem is that it can be really discouraging for your team to continually miss goals. My rule of thumb is I should be 80 percent confident I can pull it off. In general, if you're hitting less than 90 percent of your quarterly or annual goals, you need to remove one goal next cycle to make everything else more doable. If you hit 100 percent, then you can add one more goal.
2. **Setting bad/dumb goals.** Sometimes you set a goal that is dumb, becomes irrelevant, or won't actually take you closer to your vision. As soon as you realize this is the case, rewrite it or replace it. Don't let it live on in no-man's land.
3. **Ignoring goals after you write them.** If you never look at your goals, they won't magically get done. (Luckily the next area we'll talk about is daily, weekly, quarterly, and annual habits, which include reviewing goals.)
4. **Creating overly complex goals.** Keep your goals clear and simple. You should be able to recite them from memory. For example, "50 Percent Financial Freedom 2024" is our title for our financial goal.

Once you have agreed on a financial goal, have a go at the other capitals: intellectual, relational, physical, and spiritual. This is going to become a core competency of your family team, so get used to setting goals and knocking them out!

Next, we are going to look at how to make these goals a reality.

ACTION PLAN

This is the final step of setting your direction. It is the connection point between dreams and reality.

- Start by setting family goals that bridge your vision and current reality, focusing on achievable, clear actions that align with your mission and values.
- Use the S.M.A.R.T. acronym to structure each goal, making sure it's specific, measurable, assignable, realistic, and time-related.
- Once comfortable with one capital, apply this approach across all five of them: financial, intellectual, physical, relational, and spiritual.

AREA 3

MEETINGS

Almost without exception, all well-run modern organizations operate on cadences tied to years, quarters, weeks, and days. While these structured time frames existed earlier, they were formalized in the mid-twentieth century by experts such as Peter Drucker and consulting firms such as Boston Consulting Group. As organizations became more complex and the need for coordination increased, these rhythms helped bring order to the turmoil.

I think regular family meetings are pretty common, but their frequency and content vary widely from home to home. Chandler and I have spent thirteen-plus years perfecting our process, and more than any other tools in this book, our family meetings have made a huge impact in bringing order and clarity to an otherwise chaotic reality.

Why Do Regular Meetings Help Quell Chaos So Well?

1. Clarity. By prompting regular review of the things that matter—numbers, mission, vision, values, goals, and so

on—these cadences force the most important things to the forefront of our attention. It's easy to get confused in the jungle of day-to-day life. It's helpful to helicopter up regularly to make sure we're still going the right way. In our family, we *said* our mission was about having a cultural impact, but last year that wasn't present at all in our life. Thus, this year we started working on this book because we think it's the highest impact thing we can do to help the world with what we've been given.

2. **Accountability.** This is huge. For me personally, knowing that I will be asked at a specific time if I did the thing I said I would do is extremely motivating. I need other people within my family to check back with me and hold me to my commitment to schedule that appointment or do that chore for the good of the family.
3. **Visibility.** You can't lead what you don't see. For us, with seven kids, it's easy to miss how a specific kid is doing in their education, relationships, health, and so forth. Regularly surfacing all the components of an organization ensures that we don't neglect the things that slip out of sight and out of mind.
4. **Space.** Urgency has a tendency to trump everything. The problem is, if we spend all of our time doing only the things that are urgent, we'll never get to the more important actions that will help us avoid the urgent problems in the first place. Having a regular cadence to focus on the most important things—not just the most urgent—is crucial to making real traction.
5. **Communication.** If you have strong leaders on your team, it's inevitable that you, your spouse, and your children will start running in different directions. Being autonomous is important to making progress, but you also need to regularly check in with the team as a whole to get the most impact

from working together. I could go on and on, but I find it pretty fascinating that the Securities and Exchange Commission (SEC) and other government regulatory bodies literally require specific annual and quarterly rhythms for all publicly traded companies. Even nonprofit organizations have annual and quarterly financial requirements. The same should be true for families, as I believe it is a requirement for a well-functioning family team.

Family Meetings

I first learned about family meetings from my mentor, Jeremy Pryor. He was the CEO of an agency called Epipheo, and we became friends when my son was born in 2012. At the time, Jeremy had five young children, ran a company of seventy people, and still had time to do real estate and nonprofit work as well. In my new roles as a father and startup CEO, I reached out to him to see if we could hang out so I could learn how he did it all.

What I learned from observing Jeremy's life has impacted me more than anything else in my adult life. He had the same level of organizational leadership—and energy—in his home that he had in his business. He ran a weekly "business meeting" with his wife and older kids where he checked in on their goals, habits, and commitments for each week. He took his family on annual off-sites where they dreamed about where they wanted to go and made major strategy shifts based on those dreams. As a person who draws a lot of energy from business leadership, I felt like I'd finally found my way, and I realized I could use these business tools in my home as well.

Adding Meetings into Family Life

When Chandler and I first started implementing weekly, quarterly, and annual meetings, they were long, boring, and clunky. It wasn't natural for us to translate this business stuff into a family setting. I have to give credit to Chandler for her patience as we worked together to figure out how to make it function best for our family.

Over time, we've developed the lightest set of meetings that still drive the clarity and effectiveness we need. We break them into a daily stand-up meeting, weekly business meeting, quarterly off-site meeting, and annual retreat. I know that probably sounds like a lot, but if you follow the steps and implement one at a time, it really is very doable.

Let's get into each one.

CHAPTER 11

The Daily Stand-Up

The concept of the daily stand-up meeting is attributed to Ken Schwaber and Jeff Sutherland, inventors of the "Scrum" framework in the early 1990s. The idea was that at the beginning of each day, before engineers could get into their deep work, they would all stand in a circle and answer three questions:

1. What did you do yesterday?
2. What will you do today?
3. Are there any impediments in your way?[1]

The reason they wanted to do this "Daily Scrum" meeting standing up was to keep it as brief as possible. They figured no one would want to hold a two-hour meeting while standing, so out of simple discomfort, folks would keep it short.

In our family, it's definitely less *work*-oriented, but we've found the daily stand-up incredibly helpful for starting our day all on the same page. We do it every weekday morning, and we cover the agenda for the day, answer any questions, and make sure anyone communicates if they need anything (e.g., a paper edited) to hit a deadline.

The goal of the daily stand-up is to quickly sync everyone up by making sure everyone is aware of what's going on and to address any interruption requests upfront to minimize disruptions later in the day.

When I first instituted daily stand-ups in my company, we had maybe ten people overall, so we did the stand-up in the main gathering room in our office. Anywhere will do, but at home, we do this in our kitchen.

The main mistake I made at work—and one I think a lot of leaders make—was using the daily stand-up as an accountability meeting. I was most interested in ensuring we were making progress toward our goals, so I saw this as an opportunity to hold everyone's feet to the fire and push for traction. This approach created some discomfort or dread around the meeting and undermined the autonomy of team members. In reality, if you have to check in daily with your teammates or employees to make sure they're making progress, there is something pretty wrong. Later on, I learned to be more of an observer and let the team talk through their progress.

One huge benefit I found from daily stand-ups that I didn't expect (and maybe wasn't intended) was its cultural effect on the team. Circling up and seeing each other every single day really started to create a group culture. In addition to the usual questions, we started doing silly things like throwing in a "Would you rather" question or asking everyone about their favorite TV show. This built a level of camaraderie and group identity unlike other tools I've seen. Once our company grew so large we had to split into multiple daily stand-ups, I really missed those moments.

How It Works at Home

Very simply, we do our daily stand-up over breakfast as we all eat together around the table. It helps us get on the same page, focus on the same things, and start the day as a team. Here is what we typically do:

- Chandler shares the plan for the day with everyone. We align on the calendar and discuss any driving logistics and anything else the kids need to be prepared for.
- As soon as Chandler finishes the plan for the day, the kids raise their hands with questions. It's like a press conference, and Chandler will call on one kid at a time. Questions might range from "What's for dinner?" to "Can we stop at the store and get cat food after choir?"
- I give the kids a quick directive of what they should do next, such as, "Everyone, please calmly clear your dish, brush your teeth, and head down to your desk to start school in five minutes."

Having a simple way to touch base every single morning has definitely started to shape our family. We have a collective awareness of what everyone is up to, and we feel like a united team interacting together.

Obviously, breakfast may not work for everyone; it might make more sense for your family to do an evening stand-up after dinner or have an asynchronous check-in via text message. No matter the time or place, getting everyone on the same page will make a huge difference, both culturally and logistically.

> Morning stand-ups have been an awesome addition to our meeting cadences, especially as our kids are getting a little older and more autonomous. They want to know what their day holds, what they're having for dinner, when they have free time, and so on. But don't read this and picture a sleek corporate meeting. There is usually someone fussing or a seven-year-old who raises their hand with a thoughtful question like "BURRRRRPPPP!" Yes, these are tools for your family, but remember

that your kids are still kids. You can use this time to teach and train them how you expect them to behave, and with daily repetition they will get more and more used to it. But if it feels more like *Lord of the Flies* than *The Social Network*, you're not necessarily doing it wrong; you may just have a young family. Keep at it, and over time it will become an essential point of daily connection for your family.

Meeting Tips

- **Less is more.** It's tempting to let this thing creep bigger and bigger. *Don't*. Short and sweet is what you're going for here—not one big, heroic effort once a month.
- **It won't "hit" everyone.** With the age span of our kids, no matter what we say, something will be over someone's head or below their ability. I used to worry about this, but I've come to accept that it's good for kids to get used to *not* being the intended target for every communication or topic. They're still learning a lot by being included.
- **Teens really benefit.** Once you add some drivers or teenagers with their own schedules, getting on the same page is a huge deal to prevent arguments before they happen.

Give it a shot for a week and see if the daily stand-up creates more clarity, order, and culture in your family!

ACTION PLAN

Try starting a daily stand-up with these simple steps:

- **Share the plan.** Over breakfast (or another time that works for you), have one parent go over the day's agenda, plans, and logistics.

- **Answer questions.** Let everyone ask quick questions to clarify anything about the day.
- **Set next steps.** Give each family member a small directive, like clearing the dishes or getting ready for school.

CHAPTER 12

The Weekly Meeting

We all know we *should* do a weekly meeting. Realistically, though, things get busy, and we end up checking our calendars at 10 p.m. on Sunday night just to make sure we don't miss anything major. So, how do we fit in a weekly meeting?

It's worth noting that a weekly business meeting is one of the few (or only) meetings that make the cut in startups. If you run a good company, you become ruthlessly efficient in these meetings and use them to drive clarity and decision-making before getting right back to work.

The Wrong Way

First, let's talk briefly about common ways I've seen people make weekly meetings totally suck and how to avoid repeating those mistakes.

1. **Boring meetings.** When I introduce the idea of a weekly business meeting for families to people who work in larger organizations, they immediately roll their eyes and say, "Please,

no more boring meetings." Let me be really clear: A good weekly meeting should be high energy and high conflict—like great television. It should be dynamic and feel like the most productive hour of the week.

The main reason I've seen boredom in these meetings is politics. By politics, I mean people either saying unimportant things or not saying important things in order to gain status. A lot of this comes from a company's culture—if they don't value truth-telling at all levels, then, yes, meetings will become boring. Collaborative truth-telling under the gun is what we're shooting for. If you're looking to start weekly meetings in your company or your family, make sure you set this vision clearly.

2. **Sporadic meetings.** Sometimes you might skip a few weeks and then get back to it every once in a while. This is a disaster. If everyone can't trust that we'll meet every week at the same time and same place to cover the same things, we'll start trying to cram too much into these meetings—or even worse, we'll need to schedule one-off meetings the rest of the week, which will torpedo productivity. A well-run hour each week at the same time could save ten hours of random meetings during the rest of the week.
3. **Long meetings.** Related to a boring meeting is a meeting that is too long. These are typically the result of poor time management by the meeting's leader or ignoring the scheduled stop time because the topic feels "too important."

   The role of the leader in the meeting is to steward what we talk about and when. (This is yet another good reason to select a leader.) They should regularly cut people off and say, "Yes, that is important, but let's save it for the right point in the meeting," or "Although that is a good point, we need to stay on topic here." There is a finesse to pacing a meeting, and it's a crucial role to serve the greater good.

As long as you have the same meeting at the same time every week, there should be no issue with circling back to a topic if you run out of time. Everyone needs to trust that the meeting will start and end on time, every time. Having a rhythm like this in a family will help eliminate scheduling conflicts, interruptions, and so on.

4. **Angry meetings.** On the far end of the spectrum, away from boring meetings, are some organizations where it feels like each week's meeting is a fight. I am sure many of you have experienced this. Please don't fight in the meeting. Go back to the relational or big-picture sections of this book, work through those, and then get back to the work. If you realize there is a relational issue bubbling up, especially if you have an older kid who seems to be opposing everything you say, don't fight it out there. Get through the meeting and then schedule some 1-on-1 time to explore what's going on.

Getting It Right for Your Family

Here are the essential details to cover:

1. **Who.** If you're brand-new to weekly meetings, I recommend starting with just you and your spouse. Over time, I think older kids should participate as well, but you want to keep it from becoming entertainment for younger kids. This is a working meeting for the thriving of the family, so keep it as small as possible for those who can actually shape the family's direction. A good rule of thumb is one can join the meeting once they have a family credit or debit card. When my kids are around sixteen years old, I'll invite them. I know other people who invite their kids sooner, but I just want everyone involved to be a real decision-maker.
2. **Where.** Ideally, you'll do this meeting with a whiteboard nearby. You want it to be free from distractions, so if you

have a young family, leaving the home or having the meeting when kids are preoccupied is a necessity. In a bind, we've had our weekly meetings in the car on long road trips, outside, and even via Zoom. The important thing is to have no distractions.

3. **When.** This is the trickiest part. You need to find a time when you are both alert and free. If you have a young family (like us), this can be incredibly difficult. Times that have worked for us over the years have been:
   - 11 a.m. on a weekday: My mother-in-law comes over and helps with our homeschool while Chandler and I lock ourselves away in my home office.
   - 2 p.m. on a Sunday: After we put the kids down for naps, Chandler takes a quick fifteen-minute snooze while I prep the numbers. Then we quickly work through everything. It's less than ideal because kids can wake up, but it's still better than nothing.

We have tried evenings too, but I just hate that. By the end of the day, I'm too exhausted to think clearly, and I tend to get more emotional when I'm tired. You have to find what works for you and stick to it.

Like in work meetings, it's useful to have a leader—yes, even if there are just two of you in the family meeting. Take turns if you like, but I suggest having the CEO lead this meeting. I've found that when I lead, I actually talk less. The format requires you to usher the conversation along, which naturally makes it weird for you to talk too much.

Weekly Meeting Outline

Without further ado, let's get into the structure of your weekly meeting. It's a sixty-minute session, and I'll break it out by estimated time. (If you can only do thirty minutes, that's fine—anything is better than nothing.) Let's go!

Introduction: Start with gratitude and connection. (5 minutes)

I try to start our meeting with a solid hug and a little-too-long kiss. It's a good reminder that yes, this will be a productive meeting, but it's a productive meeting with my romantic partner. Productivity is a dimension of our relationship, not its entirety.

We ask each other, "What do we have to be grateful for in the past week?" For example:

- Our local swim club is open for the summer.
- Our kids are loving swim team.
- The weather is beautiful.
- The garden is coming in nicely.
- We had multiple touchpoints with friends this week.
- We're all healthy.

Writing such things down and looking at the list really helps frame our emotions and set the tone. We're going to spend a bunch of time problem-solving in the next hour, so it's good to remember the things that are working well and not just focus on what's broken.

1. Review last week's to-dos. (5 minutes)

(If this is your first meeting, this doesn't really apply yet, but it will next time.) Go through each task one by one and ask, "Did we complete this task?" If so, cross it off. If not, ask, "Do you/we/I commit to do this in the next seven days?" If so, move it to next week's list. If not, then kill the task. You don't want tasks you no longer believe in or can't accomplish to muddy up the list.

You don't have to list tasks you do every week like "mow the lawn" or "cook dinner"; rather, these are specific tasks you commit to doing in response to a number that is off or an issue that is brought up.

> We use a spreadsheet and just create a new column for each new week that we meet. I've found this to be really impactful. When you can scroll through and see your previous meetings all in one place, it helps you gain perspective on the progress you've made. It also makes you feel like you've really accomplished something. Our spreadsheet dates back five years, and it's kind of fun to go back and see what we were dealing with in the past.

2. Review your goals. *(5 minutes)*

This is where you check in on the goals you set in the goals chapter (or in the upcoming quarterly meeting chapter). Briefly go through each goal and simply say one of the following:

- "On track."—This means you have high confidence you will complete the goal by its deadline.
- "On edge."—This means if something doesn't change, you may not be able to hit the goal. This should become an issue to discuss, but don't explain it now.
- "Off track."—This means unless something changes, you will *not* complete the goal. It's absolutely mandatory for this goal to become an issue.

This process should take less than five minutes. It's so tempting to explain the status of each goal and share your progress, but don't do it yet.

3. Review your calendar and budget. *(5 minutes)*

Warning: This step can take up way too much time. Be careful.

Chandler and I quickly review the next two weeks of the calendar to make sure we're on the same page. If a longer discussion is needed, kick it down to the next section. All you want to do here is call out anything abnormal in the calendar or fill each other in if you're missing anything.

After reviewing the calendar, we look at our account balances or budget categories and make sure we're generally on track. Note: If you're a budgeting family with categorization, you have to categorize *before* the meeting. All you should do here is give each other a heads-up if you're getting close or going over on any given category. Again, don't get pulled into a long conversation here—it's just a quick check.

4. Problem-solve any issues. (35 minutes)

All right, you've ticked off the necessary but slightly boring stuff. Now you get to the *point* of the meeting. This is what you're here for—to solve problems!

If you can only implement ONE thing from this entire book, I believe spending time solving problems once per week will fundamentally change your family's life, even within one month of doing it.

I also believe this is one of the most tangible ways in which I show love to my family: I commit an hour a week of my clearest thinking and problem-solving ability simply for the purpose of helping my family thrive. Here's how you can make this work for you too.

STEP 1: LIST ALL THE PROBLEMS.

Take turns listing all the problems or issues you have in your family life right now. This can come from the numbers you reviewed, your goals, or something that popped up during the week. It can be big and existential, or it can be petty and small. For example:

- The air conditioner is dying at our duplex; should we replace it now?
- We need to book flights for a trip at the end of the summer, but our travel budget is empty. Should we pull from savings?
- Are we going to have another child?
- Our daughter wants to quit Brazilian jiujitsu, but the other kids want to keep doing it. Should we let her?
- Our friend just had surgery. What can we do to help him?
- A couple wants to come over for dinner. When can we schedule it?
- It's our son's birthday in a couple of weeks. What's the plan?

This is a catch-all list to get items out of your head and onto a whiteboard or paper you both can see.

If this is your first time doing this, your list is going to be LONG and probably overwhelming. *Breathe*. Even if it's long, I promise it has an end. Eventually, you'll run out of things to add, and that list will be all of your problems. There is something deeply calming about seeing the end of your problems.

STEP 2: PICK ONE OR TWO PROBLEMS TO SOLVE.

Each of you now gets to pick one or two things from the list that you want to solve first. I like to pick one "urgent" problem and one "important" problem. (I define *important* as something that, if solved now, would make other problems easier or irrelevant.)

When you're doing this, try your best not to operate from only your own point of view but from your family's point of view as a whole. Which problem, if solved, would most help your family?

Don't worry if you're having trouble narrowing it down—if you knock those two out quickly, you can go back to the list for more. Or, worst-case scenario, you just come back in seven days and do it again.

Got your two problems each? Great, let's move to step 3.

STEP 3: UNDERSTAND THE PROBLEM.

This is where it gets good. You need to break down the problem by using analysis tools. One of you (perhaps the CEO) reads the problem out loud. The person who identified the problem explains more about it. Together, you brainstorm answers to the following questions:

1. **Comparison.** How does this problem compare to other similar problems? Other families?
2. **Circumstances.** What else is going on that may be contributing to this problem?
3. **Relationship.** What causes the problem? What precedes it or follows it?
4. **Authority.** What have the people whom we see as authorities on the topic said about it?
5. **Rephrase.** The person who did *not* bring up the problem must rephrase it in a sentence or two so that the person who raised the problem can say, "Yes, that is the problem."

Let's do an example.

Problem: Our oldest son is causing fights with his youngest siblings.

- *Definition.* What do you mean by *fights*?

  His sister will be doing art by herself, and he'll walk by and say something critical for what seems like no reason. So I guess I'd define it as an argument—or even just picking on her verbally.

- *Comparison*. How does this problem compare to other problems we've had?

  This feels more low level than rifts he's had with his siblings in the past with deep hurt. It feels more like pestering than coming from bitterness or anger.
- *Circumstances*. What else is going on that may be contributing to this problem?

  I think he's sleeping a little less right now because he's been staying up reading this book he's really excited about. Also, now that school is out, I think he's a little bored. He is supposed to be adopting a new hobby (wood carving) for the summer, but I think he lost his whittling knives, so he's given that up.
- *Relationship*. What is causing this?

  He's totally bored. Also, I think he's reading *Calvin and Hobbes* right now and finds the attitude in that funny, so he may be mirroring some of that.
- *Authority*. What do people we respect say about this?

  I think your mom said that boys need to sweat first thing in the day to be sane people.
- *Rephrase*. Okay, so let me give this a shot: "Our oldest son is tired and bored, and he's picking verbal fights to entertain himself. This is because he's sleeping less, has less to do, and really doesn't have a better use of his time, yes?"

  Yes, that's it.

Now you can move to the last step.

STEP 4: SOLVE THE PROBLEM AND CAPTURE NEXT STEPS.

If you love solving problems, you likely already have a million solutions to this problem ready to go. That's what you're looking for—you and your partner should have defined the problem so well in step three that the solution is just jumping off the page.

Now all you need to do is propose some solutions to the problem and talk through the lowest effort/highest impact solution.

- For tiredness: Let's hold fast that he needs to stop reading by 9 p.m. We used to have that rule, and we've gotten lax on that.
- For boredom: It sounds like we should buy the whittling equipment he needs for his summer hobby.
- For energy: Swim team starts this week, so he'll likely be more tired after doing that every morning.

Next steps:

- Blake: Tonight, I'll remind him about the lights-out rule.
- Chandler: I'll buy the whittling tools he needs.

Make sure those next steps are written down, and move on to the next problem!

Like any skill, this formal process may feel a little awkward at first. Also, to be fair, some problems don't need to be fleshed out in this much detail. If you think you've got it, feel free to skip through some elements. However, if you find yourself not aligning or struggling with solutions, you can go back to the structure and work through it.

Mapping out and solving problems is one of the most important skills you can have as a human being. Commit as a couple to becoming world-class problem-solvers. It will help you in every area of your family life.

5. Capture to-dos and rate the meeting. **(5 minutes)**

Quickly make sure you've captured all the next steps, which are now your to-dos for the week. Are they all there? Do you mutually commit that you're going to do those things? Great!

Now, very briefly ask each other, "On a scale of one to ten, how effective was this meeting?" If you score it lower than an eight, follow up with, "What's one thing we could do differently next week to make it better?" Over time, this will help you get better and better at meetings. It's a skill that takes practice, and it's worth seeking feedback and continuously improving.

After all that, share a high five and a hug and get back to your day!

Congratulations—you are well on your way to creating order out of the chaos of family life.

Meeting Tips

- **Stick to it.** Even if you have to move stuff around and do a thirty-minute meeting before bed, make the effort. A short meeting is better than no meeting.
- **Don't combine weekly meetings with date night.** I know it seems like it would make so much sense—you already have childcare, and you could just do a date/meeting combo or add it at the beginning or end. Believe me, we've tried. It just doesn't work. You end up feeling sorry for yourself the whole business meeting or doing business the whole date night. Maybe you can figure it out, but I don't know anyone who has pulled this off.
- **Keep it playful.** I heard this great quote from John Cleese about playfulness: "The very essence of playfulness is an openness to anything that may happen, a feeling that whatever happens, it's ok."[1] By keeping a playful tone, you can reassure your partner that you're going to be okay no matter what problem you are dealing with.

I think those are all my tips for now. I really hope this serves your family like it has mine. We are the fruit of our decisions, and to create space to make the best decisions you can is one of the greatest acts of love you can give your family. May you be unified with your spouse and bravely make big moves—even mistakes—as you learn, grow, and try again together.

> I've found that if I don't capture issues when I notice them throughout the week, it's hard for me to remember all of them when we sit down to have our weekly meeting. So I keep a page in my planning notebook where I list issues whenever I encounter them. They're often tied to times when I've felt higher emotions or stress.
>
> Example: When it's time to get in the car, all our kids scatter, and I feel like I'm rounding up kittens to get them out the door on time. I end up frazzled and late, and I'm a grumpy mom in the car. I also want to pack them up less often because it's stressful.
>
> When I can just jot such issues down in a running list I know I can pull out during our weekly meeting, it reminds me that this problem will get addressed, and it keeps me from giving in to the urge to vent or complain to Blake at the end of the day when we're both tired.

ACTION PLAN

Start your weekly check-in for alignment with these quick steps:

- **Start with gratitude and connection.** Begin the meeting by sharing what you're each grateful for from the past week.
- **Review tasks and goals.** Go over last week's to-dos and check on any family goals, noting if they're on track or need adjusting.
- **List problems and solve one or two.** Each of you list problems to tackle and then work together to solve one or two of them, capturing any next steps for next week's to-dos.

Additional Resources

Try our e-course for weekly family meetings or buy our Family Framework Meeting Journal at TheAllsmiths.com.

CHAPTER 13

Quarterly Off-Sites

Getting away for a half day every quarter to evaluate your progress and set your intention for the next ninety days is standard practice in any well-run organization—and it works really well in family life too.

Maybe you've already noticed this, but when you go on vacation or otherwise disrupt your daily pattern, that's often where you'll get insight. I was on vacation when I first started imagining what would eventually become my first company. We were four hours into our drive when Chandler and I started talking about what it could be like. Just a few hours out of the office, and you're hit with new ideas and perspectives. It took me years to realize I could actually schedule and intentionally plan space away for the purpose of getting fresh perspective.

Here are the main benefits of getting away every ninety days:

- **Pattern disruption.** There are all sorts of studies that show if you want to get new ideas, you need to go to new places. This is why I prefer doing off-sites in new locations versus returning to the same coffee shops or office spaces.

- **Space to reflect.** By intentionally creating space to reflect, you can keep yourself from continuing in unhelpful patterns or repeating old mistakes.
- **Time to solve big problems.** Sometimes you have a problem that is just too big for a weekly meeting. You can stockpile these for your quarterly off-site. I like to create a big list of "open loops"—decisions that need to be made—and tick them off one by one during the problems section of the quarterly off-site. Some open loops we've tackled include "Should we have another kid?" "Should we start a new sport for the kids?" and "Should we change education options?"
- **Establish goals.** There is something about the ninety-day goal that is just right. A monthly goal is great, but there is only so much time to get things done. The ninety-day goal is short enough that you can't ignore it but also long enough that you can actually dedicate some serious effort toward traction.
- **Check in on annual goals.** Annual goals are still really important. However, by breaking them up into quarterly chunks, you can always have something manageable you're working toward. Reading twenty books a year is an essentially useless goal. But five books a quarter? Now we're talking.

Let's just jump into the tool itself—I think that will best help you see the benefits of each component.

How This Works for Your Family

Before we jump into the outline, there are some logistics to work through:

1. **Where.** I really do recommend going off-site—out of your home—for this meeting. You want to have a place you can camp out for several hours without distractions. My wife and I switch it up each off-site, so we've done coffee shops, picnic tables at a park, a hotel lobby, local startup gathering spaces, breweries, and so on. Try to have it at a place you enjoy being to keep it from feeling like too much drudgery.
2. **When.** This will have to be a bit of a compromise between what you can do with childcare and work schedules, but generally, I like a half day. I'm sharper in the morning, so we try to start by 8:30 a.m. and go until lunch. Then we eat, head home, and relieve the sitter. We've done afternoon into evening as well. I like to meet first, then share a meal after—kind of like a bonus date at the end of some hard work.
3. **Who.** If you're just starting out, I recommend just you and your spouse. Our kids haven't "graduated" into the meeting yet, but I hope someday they'll be able to join us as well. However, it'll have to be when they're mature enough that we don't feel like we need to water down the content. This is a real work meeting.
4. **How.** Let's talk about the vibe a bit. The weekly meeting is mostly just business. The annual meeting that we'll cover next is far more big-picture, visionary, and romantic. The quarterly off-site is somewhere in between. I picture it as being a peaceful breath for a second: We get our bearings, remember what's important, and then get back to work. It definitely feels like a momentary pause versus a big, reflective excursion. The leader of the meeting should try to do some little things to make it feel special, such as choosing a place you both like, getting a snack or drink you both enjoy, bringing new writing materials, or reading a quote that reminds you of what's important. These things show this is a time that is set apart from the rest of your daily life.

Quarterly Off-Site Agenda

Now that we've got that out of the way, let's get into the agenda. The meeting is generally four hours long, broken up by section. At the end of each section, take a break to stretch your legs and, if necessary, respond to any messages. When you're in each section, screens should be off and out of the way so you're 100 percent focused on the task at hand. Here we go.

Intro (15 minutes)

For the kickoff, you'll answer three quick questions. Just like the weekly meetings, begin with gratitude:

1. **What's the best news from the last ninety days?**

   There's no right or wrong way to answer the question—it's just meant to get you in a grateful, big-picture mindset. Take two or three minutes and make a list together. During our most recent off-site, Chandler and I listed these items:

   - Our kids did great in their final exams in homeschool.
   - We had a family reunion in Hocking Hills.
   - We made some new investment decisions.
   - My oldest and I had a great trip to Austin, Texas, with friends.
   - Our weekend rest rhythm has been awesome.
   - We did a great job hosting people every week.

Now, separately, create two lists in a journal or on a piece of paper to answer these questions:

2a. **What's working in our family?**

2b. **What's *not* working in our family?**

Set a timer for five minutes and write whatever comes to mind for each list. Personally, I've liked using these questions as journal prompts the week leading up to the meeting, so I often come with my lists already made. After the five minutes end, share your lists with each other and combine briefly. There's no need to answer anything; it's just helpful to see where both of you are. Here are some examples from our last off-site:

- Working
  - We didn't have to go out of pocket to pay our taxes this year.
  - Our business has steadily been providing what we need.
  - Our budgeting has greatly improved.
  - Health-wise we're all doing well, both with exercise and diet.
  - Our marriage is strong and trusting.
  - We have an overall positive family dynamic at home.
  - Our extended community friendships have really strengthened the past year.
  - Spiritually, we feel like our faith is playing a central role at home.
- Not Working
  - We're still recovering from some big financial moves we made the past couple of years.
  - Our long-term savings plan for college and retirement feels off.
  - We haven't adequately saved for "big expenses" like home repair and travel.
  - Two of our kids need more challenge intellectually.
  - We need more read-aloud time as a family.
  - Chandler's energy is feeling low post-miscarriage.
  - One of our kids needs an energy outlet during the week.

- Big emotions and high energy post-breakfast are creating chaos.
- We have some inconsistent scheduling and overlap with extended family.
- We feel like we could do more for some people in our community.

The third question should only take a minute. One at a time, share with the other person:

3. **What are your expectations for this meeting?**

   There are no right or wrong answers here. It's important to note where the other person is and try your best to make sure that no matter what, you leave the meeting accomplishing what both persons hope or expect. For our last meeting, Chandler and I said:

   - Establish this quarter's goals.
   - Have a clear picture of what we need to accomplish.

That's pretty much it. It's kind of a lot for just fifteen minutes of introductory time, so if you need more time to process, I'd recommend using these questions as journaling prompts the week before.

Previous Quarter Review (15 minutes)

The next section is to quickly look at the key numbers and goals you set for the last quarter and see how you did. You should have already prepared these numbers before the meeting, so it should just be a quick review. Resist the temptation to dive in too deep—just say "Complete" or "Incomplete."

We'll detail what quarterly goals look like in a minute. For now, if this is your first meeting, you can just skip this section. (Congratulations, you're ahead of schedule!)

Big Picture Review (30 minutes)

Remember all the big-picture stuff like the values, mission, and vision statements you did before? It's important to revisit these every ninety days or so to refresh yourself on what matters most and create an opportunity to edit or adjust them.

1. **Refresh.** Read every element of your values, vision, and mission out loud. It's nice to pause at each section and reinforce it. When Chandler and I do this, we'll often say things like "That's right!" or may even comment briefly on areas that we feel have been more or less alive lately in our home life.
2. **Edit or adjust.** After you read each section, ask each other, "Is this still true for us?" It's okay from time to time to add or subtract a value, rephrase the vision, or (probably less often) adjust the mission. We're all still works in progress, and it's important not to be so stuck on what you've written before that it's no longer relevant. Changing the big picture all the time will cause chaos, but revisiting it every quarter will keep it fresh and relevant.

Set Quarterly Goals (30–60 minutes)

All right, you're an hour in. Stand up, stretch, and re-caffeinate, because now it's time to get into the real meat of the off-site: setting your quarterly goals.

Through this process, you will create a handful of measurable goals that will push you closer to your big picture. Similar to other exercises we've done in this book so far, you'll start with separate journaling and then Keep-Kill-Combine until you get a small list of the most important items. Let's walk through each step.

1. **List all possible goals to accomplish in the next ninety days.**
   Each of you writes down all possible goals you could tackle this next quarter. Here are some prompts to help you along:

- Read your vision. What could you realistically do in the next ninety days to move you closer to the big picture?
- Read your "what's not working" section from the beginning of this meeting. Which problem could you fix in the next ninety days?
- Thinking of your family as a whole, what could you do in the next ninety days that would make everything else easier or unnecessary?
- If this quarterly off-site happens after your annual meeting, look at your annual goals. What can you do in the next ninety days to get closer to those goals?

Use bullet points to make your list—the more, the better. Spend a solid twenty or thirty minutes on this task until you feel like you've got a neat and consolidated list. If you have time, add a star to the ones you think are the most important.

2. **Do Keep-Kill-Combine.**

Similar to what you've done in other meetings, read both of your lists aloud and write everything on a whiteboard or sheet of paper.

- **Keep.** Put a star or dot next to the goals you each individually think are the most important.
- **Kill.** Now the painful part: If neither of you thinks an item is most important, then you probably won't address it this quarter. Make sure you're both aligned with that and set aside those items for next quarter—those bullet points won't go anywhere, I'm sure.
- **Combine.** Look for any goals that are essentially the same and combine them. I think of this as a game to see how many of the goals we come up with separately actually overlap (like reverse Boggle).

3. **Make it S.M.A.R.T.**

   Each of you should now have one goal for the next ninety days. Now it's time to make it S.M.A.R.T. (see chapter 10 for a refresher if necessary):

   - Specific
   - Measurable
   - Assignable
   - Realistic
   - Time-related

   Here are a couple examples of our goals once we polished them to become S.M.A.R.T.:

   - Blake: By 3/31, finish and implement an e-course on Airbnb on our short-term rental property.
   - Chandler: Put together a meal capsule strategy and start implementing it by 1/31, then adjust by 3/31.

You'll be revisiting these goals in your weekly meetings going forward, so keep them as short and memorable as possible.

Woo! If you got all the way through that, great job. This exercise is not for the faint of heart. We've found this is definitely a skill that takes practice, and choosing the goal itself is more than half the battle. Pat yourselves on the back and move to the last big part.

Solve Problems (30–60 minutes)

This is the exact same process we do in our weekly meetings. (If you're still new to this process, go back to chapter 12 and review it in detail.) As a reminder, here are the key steps:

1. List all the problems.
2. Pick one or two problems to solve—the ones you think are most important.

3. Understand the problem by brainstorming (definition, comparison, circumstances, relationship, authority, and rephrase).
4. Solve the problem with the lowest effort/highest impact solution.

After an hour or so of doing this, you should feel accomplished and likely exhausted. This was some serious work—well done! On to the final step.

Conclude the Meeting (5 minutes)

Before you grab food, briefly do these two things:

1. **Capture all next steps.** Review everything you did and make sure you both have a clear written list of all the next steps—not just from solving problems but also from your goals and any other discussions.
2. **Rate the meeting.** On a scale of one to ten, how did you feel it went? What's one thing you could do better next time? As always, this is a work in progress, so don't worry—it can only go up from here!

Meeting Tips

- **Come prepared.** I didn't do this really well at first, but coming prepared with numbers, journaled lists, and so on will greatly improve your experience in this meeting. If you're leading, preparation will help you focus more on facilitating versus trying to process and facilitate simultaneously. The very best scenario is one where you both journal beforehand through at least what's working and not working, and you have a chance to read each other's notes prior to the meeting. When Chandler and I do that (admittedly we don't manage it every time), it's great.

- **Commit to no phones.** For real. Put them away. The dynamic completely changes when it's just you two working on the problems undistracted. If you need to periodically check for emergencies, do it—but schedule it and make it intentional.
- **Pay attention to the vibe.** If you feel yourself getting sour or sad or starting to fight, stop and name it. Something simple like "Oh man, I think we're starting to get overwhelmed" can do wonders. It's normal to experience a range of emotions in these meetings; calling it out and putting you and your spouse on the same side of the table is crucial. You don't even need to fix anything, just call it out, maybe take a break, and then keep doing the work.
- **Treat it like work.** Take this process (not yourself) as seriously as you do your work. Dress professionally, sit professionally, and act professionally. These signals will tell you and your spouse that this is important.
- **Think about the before and after.** This meeting will take a lot of energy. As you schedule it, also think about the day or two before and the day or two after. You'll want to add in some breathing space so you can come in with energy and have some time to recover afterward.

Great job if you've read along this far—it's so rare for families to do this type of thing. By diving in, you will immensely bless your spouse, your kids, and even generations to come. Way to go doing the hard work!

> As the perfect bridge between your weekly meeting cadence and your annual meeting cadence, quarterly off-sites always feel like a breath of fresh air and a healthy dose of realignment. It's so easy to get lost in

> the weeds of the day-to-day work of family life. Taking a half day every three months to remember the mission, vision, values, and goals your family is working toward will give you new energy and keep your hearts connected.

ACTION PLAN

Kick off quarterly family off-sites with these easy steps:

- **Choose a time and place.** Schedule a few uninterrupted hours in a quiet, enjoyable spot away from home.
- **Review the past ninety days.** Start by sharing highlights and noting what's working and what's not in your family life.
- **Set quarterly goals.** Together, decide on one or two realistic goals that will make the biggest difference over the next three months.

Additional Resources

Try our e-course for quarterly family off-sites or buy our Family Framework Meeting Journal at TheAllsmiths.com.

CHAPTER 14

The Annual Retreat

All right, it's time for the big kahuna: the annual retreat! In business, the annual retreat is often driven by a need to present the board with an annual financial plan and strategy. It typically happens in December or January, and the output is normally some combination of a strategy document, a list of annual goals, and a budget to support it. You generally will assign some homework beforehand to your key executives, and then you'll go away for one to three nights or rent a location nearby.

Normally, the leader will prepare an agenda beforehand with a map of "sessions" to facilitate the conversations needed to put together the necessary documents. You'll also typically take long breaks in the day for unstructured conversations and recreation, as well as share evening meals together for bonding and further conversation. I remember feeling a mix of closeness, clarity, and exhaustion when I came back from one of these. A well-run annual retreat can be incredibly productive, both relationally and strategically.

In an annual family retreat, we're obviously not presenting to a board, but the main outputs from this meeting will still be annual goals and a renewed sense of connection. But why go to all this effort?

It's helpful to think about the purpose of a retreat as being not just what happens while you're there but also—and more importantly—what happens when you get back. This is the big difference between a vacation and a retreat. A vacation is all about what happens while you're there: the experiences, enjoyment, relaxation, and so forth. A retreat, on the other hand, is meant to be an experience that resets the organization so that when you return, you are better.

Here's how Chandler and I hope to be different when we get back from our annual retreat:

- **We're wiser.** When we set aside time to comb through the past year and identify the lessons we've learned, we help our family avoid making the same mistakes the next year. At the end of last year in my business, I realized one decision we made had lost us about $150K. *One decision*. We only caught it by doing an analysis in preparation for our annual retreat. We promptly reversed that decision, and the business has been better for it.
- **We're closer.** Working with humans is hard. We hurt each other's feelings, we misunderstand each other, and we take each other for granted. We need time away to clear the air, see each other anew, and reconnect. Scheduling time to work on stuff like this can save you months of pain, inefficiency, and heartburn. One exercise I love, which we'll go over below, is where we actually solicit things we need to change. I've seen this invitation massively improve my work and personal relationships.
- **We're more energized.** Sometimes we need to dwell on the "why" for a while and remember what our family is all about. Now, if we do this every day, we'll never get stuff

done. But once a year, just getting pumped about our family and the big picture we're going after is super helpful.

- **We're clearer.** When we are busy in daily family life, we start to lose perspective. What are we trying to do again? Why are we doing it? How will we do it? People will also begin to develop their own individual narratives that start to pull against each other. When we get back from an annual retreat, we should all be aligned and rowing in the same direction.
- **We're more focused.** Ideally, when we leave the retreat, we will have one or two areas that each of us personally needs to focus on. I had an adviser tell me one time that a team focused on one thing has an 80 percent chance of success, while a team focused on two things has an 80 × 80 percent chance of success, or 64 percent. And three things (80 × 80 × 80) have a 51 percent chance of success. The point is, we want to come away focused, streamlined, and ready to execute.

I think you get the idea: Annual retreats are super effective. Let's get into how to do one for your family.

The Annual Retreat

Here are some logistics before we get into the format itself:

1. **When.** We like to schedule our annual retreat as close to the first week of the year as possible. In *When: The Scientific Secrets of Perfect Timing*, Daniel Pink explains the "fresh start effect"—the idea that the start of a new week, month, or year gives us a clean break from our past and makes it easier to pursue meaningful change.[1] Last year we did our retreat January 3–5, and that felt about perfect. We have

some friends who do their retreat between Christmas and New Year's, and that totally makes sense to me as well. You may have more family available then to handle logistics with kids, and for older kids, it obviously helps to schedule it when they're out of school.

2. **How long.** In general, I like to have two full days of sessions. I prefer to arrive sometime the evening before, work for two full days, and then return home either that night or the next morning. Plan for two or three nights away.
3. **Where.** Chandler and I have done beachy places like Puerto Rico, Florida, and San Diego, and we've also done local Airbnbs or friends' lake houses in Kentucky or Tennessee. Your macro-location doesn't really matter, since you're spending most of the time working. However, the micro-location of the place is pretty important. Ideally, get a home—not a hotel room—where you can spread out in a living space and work comfortably all day. It's best if the home is in a walkable area so you can take breaks by simply stepping out the door.
4. **Who.** Like the other meetings, I recommend doing the first few retreats with just your spouse (versus your spouse and children). That being said, Chandler has had a baby pretty much every other year for the past thirteen years, so half the time we bring an infant with us. Also, more than any other meeting, I highly recommend doing this with another couple, especially if they have experience with annual retreats. Chandler and I have done ours with friends the past two years and really enjoyed it. I introduce each session, and then we break out and do the exercises separately.
5. **How.** Let's talk about the vibe. Similar to the quarterly offsite, this should feel about one-third productive, one-third romantic, and one-third reflective. We spend the evenings making a fancy meal, drinking a cocktail, going for a night swim, or visiting a restaurant or coffee shop. Just because we're working doesn't mean it can't be super enjoyable.

I recommend following our agenda for your first couple retreats, and then you can branch off and make it your own.

Day 1

Session 1: Check-In and Year in Review (2.5 hours with break)

First session? Let's go! To kick things off, do the **Check-In**. Ask each other, "What do you hope to get out of these next two days?"

List all your expectations and desires. In future years, you may want to augment the outline accordingly to make sure everything gets covered. Often, Chandler and I list an open loop we need to make a decision on, a desire to revisit our values, and other things like that.

Once you have your expectations and desires out of the way, move on to the **Year in Review**. The purpose of this exercise is to reexperience the previous twelve months together and try to mine as much wisdom as you can from them. As you review the past year, map out the highs and lows. I like to do this across the five capitals (see chapter 9 for a refresher) cumulatively because it can create a chart that shows which areas of life were net gains or losses over the past year.

Chandler and I open our Google Photos and our shared calendar and go through week by week to see what we can remember. If we come across something really impactful or memorable, we'll record it on the spreadsheet and assign it a "point value" between +3 and −3. Here are some examples from a past year:

- 1/15/23: We made some new friends who ended up being a big part of our life this past year. +3 both relationally and spiritually.
- 1/29/23: Blake went to a mastermind that was really life-giving. +3 relationally.

- 2/19/23: We lost a dear friend unexpectedly and suddenly after childbirth. This was very close to home and disorienting. −3 spiritually, relationally, and intellectually.
- 3/5/23: We did a trip to Death Valley with our oldest for a birthday trip. It was so fun but also exhausting to fly with him and a baby. +3 spiritually and relationally, −1 physically.
- 3/19/23: Blake spent a bunch of money on content and sales help, and it ended up not bearing a lot of fruit. −3 financially but +1 intellectually.

This exercise can be incredibly emotional. It's not uncommon for one or both of us to cry as we relive the difficult or beautiful parts of the past year. It can also make you feel like an idiot when you can see so clearly the mistakes you made. Just keep going forward; there is wisdom on the other side.

It can feel kind of random as you go, but slowly, over time, this review starts to add up and create a "shape" of the year. You can also tally all the points to see if you had a "surplus" or "deficit" in each capital.

Now my favorite part: Record any "errors in judgment" you made in the past year, and, for each one, create a "what we learned" to help you avoid it in the future. Some (painful) examples from our past year include:

- Error in judgment: We disregarded the compounded difficulty of traveling with kids, starting school, and skipping our weekly rest day. The result? We got sick and burned out.

  What we learned: Skipping more than one rest day a month risks physical injury and exhaustion. It's an "all-nighter" for your soul.

- Error in judgment: Blake was too quick to spend money against work problems.

  What we learned: Try the free/simple solution first. Don't pay for someone to do something for you; instead, pay an expert to teach you, do it, and then, only if necessary, pay for expertise to scale it.
- Error in judgment: Our anniversary trip to Italy cost about 50 percent more than we estimated.

  What we learned: Buffer 50 percent more on vacations.

You want to develop pattern recognition so you can avoid similar mistakes in the year going forward. It also helps to take these things into account as you make a plan for the next year.

The whole exercise will probably take around 90–120 minutes. You'll get a sense when you're done because there isn't much left to say about the year.

When you hit that point, take a quick break—you earned it!

Session 2: S.W.O.T. and Team Health (2 hours)

It's time to turn to the present. These two exercises will help you evaluate where your family is as a whole and how you and your spouse are doing as a team. This one can get sensitive, so try to take a third-person point of view on both the family and the marriage relationship. Try to think less like yourself and more like a third party evaluating from the outside. Here we go.

S.W.O.T.

Have you ever heard of a S.W.O.T. analysis? This process maps out your family's Strengths, Weaknesses, Opportunities, and Threats. It is one of the most famous management consultant tools for a reason: It can really help bring clarity to an organization. To begin, go through each factor.

1. **Strengths.** This is pretty straightforward; you want to map out your family's strengths. This is also useful because it lists the "superpowers" you can leverage to get momentum as a family. What are you guys really good at? What comes naturally to you that doesn't come naturally to others? Have you received feedback that you are different or strange in certain ways? Write all those elements down. These examples are from our last off-site:
   - *Vision/influence.* When we find something that we think is great, we will recruit people like crazy to join us.
   - *Industriousness/energy/capacity.* We work really hard and do hard things.
   - *Positivity.* We tend to look for fun, create a good life, and remove the bad things.
   - *Systems.* We implement systems and habits really well.
2. **Weaknesses.** Just in case you're starting to feel cocky, now list your family's weaknesses. You may notice they are "shadow sides" of your strengths. If you need help, refer back to the previous exercise and pay attention to patterns you've seen in your judgment. Here are three examples from Chandler and me:
   - *Drive/pacing/margin.* We tend to pursue the big-picture vision and stretch ourselves too thin.
   - *Optimism.* We're not always realistic about the cost in money, time, or energy.
   - *Vulnerability with peers.* We don't often show weakness, ask for help, or share doubts externally.
3. **Opportunities.** List the realistic opportunities within reach for your family. These are good things that are right outside your grasp that you could potentially capture if you're clever and focused. Some examples for us include:

- *Life, funded*. We are getting closer to financial independence—having our monthly costs covered by asset-based income.
- *Homeschool middle school/high school co-op*. We are in an amazing elementary school homeschool co-op. With a little organization and planning, we could have this persist for the entirety of our kids' education for the next eighteen years.
- *Church*. We attend a young church, and we have an opportunity to help shepherd it according to what we think would be best for the community.

4. **Threats.** Finally, list the things that are creeping on the horizon that could potentially hurt your family. Some personality types recognize threats naturally, while others (like me) require a concentrated effort to map these out. Here are some of our examples:
   - *Agency business/short-term rentals*. Markets can change really quickly, and that could hurt our current lifestyle.
   - *Community responsibility/pregnancy*. Right now, our life is very sustainable, but Chandler is healthy and not pregnant. When/if Chandler gets pregnant, we'll need to off-load a lot of responsibility to protect Chandler's energy.
   - *Teenage years*. We are on the edge of entering the teen years with our oldest kids. We do not know what will happen here, and it may drastically affect our family culture and require a lot of energy.

The second half of the S.W.O.T. analysis is to walk through four prompts to start to shape your plans for the next year:

1. Develop strategies to use your strengths to take advantage of opportunities.

2. Implement plans to use your strengths to overcome threats.
3. Create strategies to improve your weaknesses by taking advantage of opportunities.
4. Develop contingency plans to address weaknesses that can make threats a reality.

(You will address these prompts in more detail on day 2.)

For example, in prompt 1, we looked at one of our weaknesses: overoptimism, especially around money. We paired it with one of our strengths: implementing systems. We then found a simple household budgeting system and committed to following it exactly as prescribed. In this way, we're using a strength to solve for a weakness.

TEAM HEALTH

This is one of my favorite exercises of the entire annual retreat. It is incredibly vulnerable, and it's also incredibly powerful. The point of the team health exercise is to evaluate how you and your partner are doing as a team and then to commit to improving together. We do it in three steps.

1. **Score yourselves on the T.R.A.C.K. assessment.**

   High-functioning teams tend to follow a predictable pattern. You'll find five elements that show up again and again when a team is operating at a high level. I use the acronym T.R.A.C.K. to remember them:

   - **Trust.** When team members are honest, wholehearted, and transparent with each other, they lay the most important foundation for a well-functioning team. This creates safety; without it, you will struggle.
   - **Resistance.** Good teams know how to disagree without hurting each other or being hurt. I like the phrase "Doubt each other's judgment but not each other's intentions." Disagreement isn't a threat, it's a tool.

- **Alignment.** Once you've conflicted, a decision needs to be made. Great teams can debate, disagree, and then align around a plan of action—even if it wasn't your preferred choice. It's tempting to stall or sabotage, but healthy teams commit and move forward together.
- **Commitment to accountability.** We all need accountability. Great teams call each other up and follow through on what they said they'd do. It's not just management pressure; it's peer-to-peer commitment.
- **Key outcomes.** If you do the four things above, you'll get the results you're aiming for. Output matters. The scoreboard should be clear and shared.

For this exercise, each of you should score yourselves on each element as a team (not as individuals but as a unit) on a scale of −3 to +3.

−3 = Extreme Weakness

−2 = Weakness

−1 = Slight Weakness

+1 = Slight Strength

+2 = Strength

+3 = Extreme Strength

Once you've scored yourselves separately, share each score one at a time and discuss.

2. **What is your partner's most admirable trait?**

Now that you have evaluated the partnership as a whole, look at yourself as individuals. Take some time apart—ten or fifteen minutes should be fine—to reflect on and write down what you most appreciate about your partner.

What do they bring to your partnership that you really appreciate? Give it a word and then expound for a paragraph or so that explains your reasoning and offers some examples. Really speak from your heart on this one. Once you're done, take turns sharing your paragraph out loud with your partner.

Here's a (brief) example for a theme I've done for Chandler:

Chandler makes people feel loved and appreciated. For anyone in our family (myself included), when she gives affection and warmth, it will make you feel like you are loved and belong. She really is the heart of our family.

3. **One thing I really need you to start or stop doing is . . .**

   All right, now you're getting brave. Separate again and take ten minutes or so to specify the one thing you really want the other person to start or stop doing. At the front of the exercise, I like to pre-commit to Chandler that no matter what she writes, I will try with my utmost ability to do what she says. It's incredibly vulnerable to give up control for the sake of your partner, but every time I'm surprised (and often relieved) by what she asks. There is something about this exercise that deeply builds team connection. I'm excited for you to try this.

   Chandler's "Start/Stop" for me one year was "Stop rushing the kids so much." I had gotten into a bad habit of rushing the kids to get in the car, get to bed, and so on. So, for the next year, once a week I asked her, "How'd I do with rushing the kids this week?" We're not entirely rush-free in our home now, but making it her number one request really brought weight to it.

BREAK

Go take a nap or a walk—that was a *lot* to cover.

Session 3: Review Mission/Vision/Values (1.5 hours)

This session is pretty simple compared to the other sessions so far. Personally, I like to end the day on this one because it's a little lower energy. Go through the three pillars in your big picture—mission, vision, and values—and ask:

1. Is this still true?
2. Is there anything you want to change?
3. Is anything missing?

I think doing this once a year in-depth is an awesome exercise. In general, when we do this in our quarterly meetings, we keep it pretty low level, but the annual retreat is where we really make big shifts. We probably make the most changes to our vision, some changes to our values, and the least changes to our mission.

End of Day 1

This is a division point in the annual retreat. Up until now, we've been pretty high level—relationships, big picture, reflection, and so on. Day 2 is going to be increasingly tactical and tangible, and you'll want all your energy as you go into the next three sessions.

Day 2

Session 4: Create a One-Year Plan (2 hours)

The goal in session 4 is to come up with a one-year plan that gets you closer to your big-picture vision. This is how we like to do this:

1. **Look at the big-picture vision.** As you think about your vision, really imagine where you want to go as a family.
2. **Look at your S.W.O.T. analysis.** Specifically look at the opportunities that align with your big-picture vision, as well as the threats that might go against it.
3. **List all possible annual goals.** Separately, write out all the potential initiatives for the year that will get you closer to your vision.

4. **Keep-Kill-Combine.** You know the exercise by now. Put your lists together and Keep-Kill-Combine until you get to something that seems reasonable.
5. **Polish.** Do some copywriting/editing on the goals you kept to make sure they are S.M.A.R.T. and memorable.

Now, this part is new: Look at the goals you came up with and think through how this might affect your five capitals. Specifically, what capital can you spend against the goals to ensure you accomplish them?

- **Financial.** Can we budget money against these goals?
- **Intellectual.** Do we need to read books, buy e-courses, or hire coaches to help us accomplish these goals?
- **Physical.** How should our weekly rhythms, habits, or even physical space change to support these goals?
- **Relational.** Who do we know who can help us with these goals?
- **Spiritual.** How can we incorporate these goals into our spiritual practices (e.g., pray through these goals)?

Capture any next steps that come out of this exercise.

Session 5: Establish Quarterly Goals (1.5 hours)

This process is identical to what you do in a quarterly off-site.

1. List all possible quarterly goals for this upcoming quarter that map to your annual goals.
2. Keep-Kill-Combine.
3. Polish and make sure each S.M.A.R.T. goal belongs to one of you.

Session 6: Problem-Solving (1 hour)

I like to use this session to really tackle the biggest, scariest problems we're facing. Next week, you'll still have your normal weekly meeting, so you might as well go all in and tackle something BIG.

Review your threats and weaknesses from the S.W.O.T. analysis.

1. List all problems.
2. Select one or two problems each.
3. Solve by examining:
    a. Definition
    b. Comparison
    c. Circumstances
    d. Relationship
    e. Authorities
    f. Rephrase
4. Capture your next steps.

Session 7: Review Next Steps and Conclude (15 minutes)

Wow. You did it! That was a HUGE amount of work to do in two days. Now all you need to do is review everything you did and make sure you've captured your next steps.

Once you're finished, look at all you've done and take a deep breath. You have set up your family for a year of more clarity, better teamwork, and clear goals that will take you one step closer to your big-picture vision. Well done!

Meeting Tips

- **Prepare.** More than any of the other meetings, the annual retreat benefits from preparation. Having a clear plan of what you want to accomplish and being familiar with each of the exercises will greatly help you. The more comfortable Chandler and I have become with these exercises, the more we can focus on our family and less on the process. Logistically, you'll need to figure out childcare, such as swapping with another couple, going to a resort with childcare, or securing extended family.

- **Don't power through.** This retreat is supposed to serve your family—you don't have to serve *it*. If you need to spend more time on something and cut out other exercises, just do it. Especially since this retreat requires a lot of relational intimacy, it's important to flex to both of your individual needs.
- **Keep it fun.** If at any point you start to feel like this whole thing is a drag, pause and do something fun. We all have habits and cultures that shape how we approach work. Not all of life is fun, but when you're doing something big-picture and setting direction, you need to be in a positive mindset. If you're not there, be honest and make a change.

Each year will get better and better as you do this, so don't get discouraged. By putting an annual retreat in place, you are making time for your family, for your relationship with your spouse, and for yourself. Communication will improve, and you will feel more like a team than ever before. Try it!

> It's annual retreat time! This is always a highlight of our year—it's a time to connect, get on the same page, and get excited about the life we're building together. But if you have a young family, you know that sometimes the amount of work it takes to get a weekend of childcare, pack the kids' bags, pack your own bag, get sitters for pets, and then put everything back in order when you return can feel overwhelming. Be honest with yourself: This is a lot of work. It just is. But it's also 100

percent worth it. You will be so glad you spent the time/money/effort to make this happen, and your family will be blessed immensely by your hard work and sacrifices.

ACTION PLAN

Plan a meaningful annual retreat with these simple steps:

- **Choose dates and location.** Schedule two or three days at the start of the year, ideally somewhere comfortable and quiet.
- **Reflect on the past year.** Together, review your highs and lows from the past year, noting lessons learned.
- **Set annual goals.** Define one or two family goals for the year that align with your big-picture vision and establish quarterly goals to keep yourselves on track.

Additional Resources

Try out our e-course for annual family retreats or buy our Family Framework Meeting Journal at TheAllsmiths.com.

AREA 4

OPERATIONS

Now we need to focus on the tactical skills and tools necessary to run an organization. The trick with a lot of these skills is not always about being creative or innovative but rather being consistent in implementing them over the course of months and years.

When I began working in startups, I thought of myself as more of a visionary—I liked the big picture, sales, and external relationships and was kind of averse to digging into the weeds of operations. Startup culture broadly supports this idea, especially heralding visionary leaders like Elon Musk, Steve Jobs, and Bill Gates. In reality, though, most organizations really need a faithful leader who can put their head down, acquire the skills they need, and get the work done.

For me, this has been an embarrassing process of having to learn on the job with real people's careers on the line. The same is true—and even more so—when leading a family. Babies don't come with a manual. None of us start with the skills we need to get the job done. My goal in these next four chapters is to provide some basic management skills that I learned from startups and applied to my family to help create more momentum, clarity, and impact at home.

It will take practice to master each of these, so be patient and just pick one at a time.

CHAPTER 15

Build a Weekly Rhythm for Family Flow

The most precious resource we have in life is time. Ask any old rich person if they'd rather have their money or more time, and they'll always choose time. In a family, especially before kids can drive, it's crazy how fast we can all fall into using our time poorly. Just a few sports games, parties, and school events, and suddenly you're spending your life in the car—and any sense of margin has gone out the window.

How do we most effectively leverage our time to proactively build the life we actually want to have? A life that lines up with our values and drives toward our vision and mission?

There's a tool for that, and it's called the Weekly Rhythm.

Living in a Weekly Rhythm means you choose to design and then live in your ideal week, rather than simply react to what all the opposing organizations in your life want from you. It takes courage to push back—especially in the realm of family—but it is the only way to drive meaningful progress for any organization.

In startups, the core elements of the business are dictated by regular rhythms and cadences on a weekly and monthly basis:

- **Product.** Engineers and designers work through a "scrum sprint" process where they go through a regular calendar of designing, building, testing, and reviewing.
- **Marketing.** Marketers run performance marketing sprints weekly, adhere to daily and weekly content calendars, and so forth.
- **Finance.** Finance people adhere to a regular cadence of weekly and monthly tasks for billing and expenses.

The core elements of each organization are built into the regular rhythm of the entire group. As Stephen Covey says, "The key, however, is not to prioritize your schedule, but to schedule your priorities."[1] Nobody on the engineering team says, "I've just got to figure out when I can squeeze in some time for code review." It's built into the schedule because it's what they do.

Compare that with family. Can you imagine telling your kid's coach, "We're not going to make practice tonight because we want to have a family night"? Sure, you *could* say it, but you'd realize pretty quickly that you're breaking some unspoken fundamental law. In general, this is the hierarchical ranking of authority on the family calendar:

1. School
2. Extracurricular activities
3. Friends and extended family
4. Religious organizations
5. Parents (maybe, if there is anything left over)

If you embrace the tool of designing and adhering to a Weekly Rhythm, just know that all these organizations are going to protest and rebel. Some people will actually freak out—Chandler and I know because we've been living a Weekly Rhythm with our family for over ten years. Despite people's protestations, though, I promise you it is completely worth it. It will fundamentally change how your whole family views your household. Here are just a few of the benefits:

- **Progress.** Rather than try to squeeze in the things you care about most—whether that's starting a new business, serving together as a family, building something new at home, or just connecting in a difficult season—you can allocate significant chunks of time toward those priorities.
- **Agency.** There is nothing more depressing than feeling like you don't have agency in life. I think so much of the depression among parents today comes from feeling like they hate their life but can't do anything to change it. By adopting a Weekly Rhythm, you can regain a sense of freedom and agency that you can actually build the life you choose.
- **Clarity.** By living most of your week in a consistent pattern, you can recognize when something goes wrong, attribute it to a cause, and change it the next week. This creates an iterative process you can optimize to create an ideal week.
- **Energy.** You can design your week to maximize your energy. We host people on Wednesday night every week, for example, so we schedule a relaxed Thursday morning so everyone can recover. You can match the energy to the occasion and design an optimal week.
- **Margin.** Whoa—the holy grail. You can put blank, open space into your Weekly Rhythm. (Did you just start drooling over the idea of *free time*?) I promise it's not a trick—you really can have regular, consistent margin in your life.

I know you probably have a bunch of objections or questions right now, and we're going to get into them in a moment. Yes, there are definitely some significant hurdles to implementing a Weekly Rhythm, but I want to assure you up front: *It can be done.*

How NOT to Implement a Weekly Rhythm

There are two main ways to approach the process. There's the nuclear option, where you just completely turn your life upside down overnight. There's also the iterative version, where you slowly morph your weekly schedule to align with your mission, vision, values, and goals. As I'm sure you can guess by now, when I first learned about Weekly Rhythms ten years ago, I chose the nuclear option. I started with a blank spreadsheet (of course) and mapped out my ideal week in thirty-minute increments. I also did Chandler the generous service of mapping out her ideal week in thirty-minute increments. (She did not appreciate it, to say the least.)

I maybe made it a week with my calendar overhaul before it fell apart. It also probably took a year before I could speak into Chandler's calendar again. So, no, I don't recommend the nuclear option.

The process I'm going to walk you through is the iterative option, and you'll never really be "done" with it. It will, however, be sustainable.

How to Implement a Weekly Rhythm

I'm going to map out four prompts for you to use to start building your ideal week. My recommendation is to keep cycling through these prompts on a regular basis. Chandler and I do this in our weekly meetings, and later on, we make bigger changes at the quarterly off-site.

Prompt 1: What's working?

With your spouse and older kids, look at last week's calendar. (If you don't keep a calendar, print one out, map out what you did last week on it, and put it up in front of everyone. Also, you're an adult—you need to keep a calendar.)

What was really good? If you had complete control of your schedule and infinite dollars, what would you *not* change?

Great. Lock it in. If you're building your rhythm digitally, set that rhythm to repeat weekly and assign it a special color. If you have a separate calendar document, put that event on it and color it a specific way to say that it's good.

Your only assignment? Make sure you do the things that work.

Prompt 2: What's not working?

Review last week again. Circle one or two pinch points that really didn't work for your family. Look for moments of having low energy, being frantically late, or just feeling miserable. (Sometimes it helps to text your partner or make a note when you experience it.) Choose the worst one.

Now it's time to try to solve the rhythm problem. Sometimes you can't get rid of the actual rhythm, but you can manipulate other variables.

Let's say you had a long day at work, and then you had to drive the kids to choir practice. You were late and hungry, and the kids were acting crazy. You ended up using the drive as an opportunity to give a long, impassioned "sermon" on the importance of personal responsibility. (This is all hypothetical, of course.) Maybe you can't quit choir, and you definitely can't quit your job, so what might some creative solutions look like?

- Eat before you pick up the kids. Having a meal beforehand to make myself less hangry is my go-to solution.
- Change drivers. Maybe you can switch driving duties with your spouse or carpool with someone else.

- Exercise earlier in the day. Sometimes exercising will set you up with a better mood for whatever the day demands.
- Add some fun. Give yourself something to look forward to—maybe watch your favorite show while they're at choir, exercise during it, or listen to music you enjoy on the drive.
- Go to work early and leave early. It's a simple solution, but if you have flexibility in your schedule, this can give you extra time in the second half of the day.
- Pay someone to drive. You can hire a babysitter to drive your kids. I know this sounds like a rich person thing, but honestly, would you rather have the extra $20 or a good relationship with your kids?

In general, the solutions will always map to money, effort, or time. Get creative—and remember that you will come back in a week to see if it's solved. If your solution doesn't solve the problem next week, try other options until one does.

Prompt 3: Look at your goals.

Remember those quarterly goals you made at your off-site? They are the top things you can do to drive toward the life you want. It's a great idea to create rhythms within your week to support those goals.

For this prompt, create a place in your schedule that you can commit to each week to make progress on one of your quarterly goals. For example, one of my quarterly goals has been to finish the book you're reading right now. So, on my weekly schedule I have a time and place for writing. It's on my calendar, just like any other meeting I'd have for work.

You may have to say no to something else in order to create this rhythm. That's great—it means you're looking trade-offs in the eye. Saying no to a good thing in order to say yes to the most important thing is a wise (and necessary) trade.

It's tempting to go crazy on this, but just start with *one* thing. A good rule of thumb is to never add or remove more than one thing each week if you want lasting change.

Prompt 4: Look at your values.

The final thing to consider when mapping out your Weekly Rhythm is your values. Sometimes when you start getting into productivity mode, it's easy to optimize so much that you squeeze out the most meaningful, nonproductive stuff. That's what values are for—to hold us back.

So pull up your list of values alongside your Weekly Rhythm. Try to map your rhythms to your values and check to see if each value is represented. For example, our values are:

- Abundance
- Savoring
- Boldness
- Curiosity
- Playfulness
- Team
- Industriousness

I'll look at our week and ask, Do we have a rhythm that represents each of these values?

- **Abundance.** We host twice per week and have our monthly generosity dinner. Check.
- **Savoring.** Our Friday celebration dinners are pure savoring—fancy meal, good friends, candles, the whole thing.
- **Boldness.** We have a couple of big moves we're trying to make as a family; this book is a part of that. We both have points in our week mapped to these big moves.

- **Curiosity.** Hmm. In the summer I was reading a lot outside on Saturdays with the kids, but now that it's fall, we've lost that rhythm. This is an opportunity for a new rhythm for sure.

When you find a value you're not living as much right now, look to see where you could fill in a rhythm to support that value. For curiosity, I think a great rhythm could be a "reading night" or "YouTube night" once a week. Chandler and I could also explore our interests a little more, either individually or together. To do so, we would find a night of the week where that could make sense and then commit to try it out for a week and see how it goes.

Repeat

That's it! It's the hard work of refining your calendar that will, over time, align your schedule with the life you want.

I recommend doing this no more than once a week for a couple of weeks. Once you've done that, back it off to only when there is an issue and then reevaluate the rhythm as a whole every quarter.

How to Overcome Objections to Living Rhythmically

Inevitably, when you start living in a Weekly Rhythm, people are going to object. I've found that more than any other tool in this book, living rhythmically gets the most pushback. Nobody really freaks out when you announce you're going to live on a financial budget, but start budgeting your time and suddenly people have an issue. Here are some tips on how to deal with it:

1. **Extend the invitation.** Specifically for friends and family, the ideal way to introduce them to living rhythmically is to invite them into a rhythm. Once you have a couple of rhythms you're consistently doing, you can start proactively inviting

the people you love into them. The conversation can look something like this:

Hey friend/family member,

I love hanging out with you so much, and I'd love to be able to spend time with you even more regularly. Here are a few things we're already doing every single week as a family:

- *Sunday church service*
- *Wednesday night game night*
- *Friday night family dinner*

It would be so cool if we could overlap in one or two of them each week—but no pressure of course.

If you can start with an invitation, it will communicate what you want to say most: that you love them and want to spend more time with them.

When Blake and I decided to move to a place with no near neighbors (after already committing to homeschooling), we realized we needed a strategy for our family's social life so we didn't become "those homeschoolers." Over the past three years, we've embraced a strategy we call the circle. Our goal is to overlap with the people we love as many times as possible every week. We outline what our recurring weekly events are and actively recruit the people we want to be close to into those rhythms (or we join theirs). The result is that we all hang with a lot of the same people four or five times per week. Rather than continually trying to schedule one-off play dates with an expanding family, we invest in the people we overlap with the most. They are our closest community, and this practice has led to one of the richest relational periods we've experienced in our lives.

2. **Ask what is expected of you.** For sports teams, church groups, school groups, and so forth, meet with the leader and ask them to clarify what good involvement looks like on a weekly basis. (Sometimes leaders throw out every opportunity to the group, and you might think you *need* to do

everything.) We did this with our church—I met with our pastor and asked from his perspective what an ideal, active member of the church would do on a regular basis. He said, "Attend/host a home group, attend most church services, and volunteer once per month." This was so helpful. We really wanted to be a part of this community, but we also couldn't do every event. We mapped those three things into our rhythm, and we have no problem with our consciences if we can't make every one-off thing. This works for sports too. We recently met with a coach of a swim team that practices five days a week. We can't do that with the number and ages of kids we have, so I asked the coach, "How many practices per week do you think are necessary to really progress at the level you'd like to see?" He said, "Two." Now we're talking. Have the conversations with the leaders of the organizations you're a part of—if nothing else, it will give you clarity.

3. **Community is compromise.** At the end of the day, our families are not islands. We need extended family, friends, and organizations to have a fulfilling life. Much of our life can be proactively scheduled into a weekly rhythm, but some parts really can't. When your best friend needs help with something big, you should go and help them. We need to be willing to break our rhythm from time to time for the people closest in our community. The important thing is that you compromise with their rhythm and they compromise with yours. We have to all work together to overlap and create a good life. Perfection is not the goal. If you're doing rhythm right, you will get pushback. If you can meet that pushback intentionally and with an openness to compromise, you can create a life with deeper relationships in all your social circles. This has definitely been the case for us, and I hope it will be for you as well.

Living in a Weekly Rhythm feels like a magic bullet to living the kind of life you actually want to live. And in a lot of ways, it really is. You can build time into your rhythm for the things you truly value and want to spend your time on. But like Blake mentioned, it can be really offensive to the most well-meaning family and friends. There is a lot of time baked into our Weekly Rhythm for what many people would call "nothing"—reading a book at home together as a family once a week, watching an episode of *Survivor* together weekly, practicing a weekly twenty-four hours of rest. None of these things feel productive or like anything special in our culture, but for our family, these pockets of time are where the deepest connection happens. They are indispensable.

But when someone is trying to schedule something, it feels really weird to respond, "Oh man, we won't be able to make that because it's *Survivor* night." (Awkward pause.) So let me just give you freedom not to give a reason you can't do something. It's okay to say, "We won't be able to make that, but here are two other dates that do work for us." You don't have to explain. And as you live more and more in a Weekly Rhythm, your friends and family will just get used to you doing things a little differently than everyone else does. Hopefully over time they'll see the fruit in your family and life.

ACTION PLAN

- **Lock in what works.** Keep one or two routines that already feel smooth, like family dinners or a regular bedtime.
- **Tweak what doesn't work.** Identify one stress point in your week (like rushed mornings) and try one small change to improve it.
- **Add one goal-focused routine.** Choose one current family goal (like more reading time) and reserve a specific time for it weekly.

CHAPTER 16

Streamline Routines with SOPs

The number one operational tool in the tool belt for any founder of a business is the Standard Operating Procedure (SOP). An SOP is a one- or two-page document that outlines exactly how to do a specific job. It can sometimes just be a checklist of exactly what to do—in order—to accomplish a task.

In a family, we're often unsure if things are chaotic because people don't know what to do or because they know what to do and don't do it. A well-written SOP can drive clarity and accountability, even with young kids.

The classic SOP example comes from McDonald's. Ray Kroc broke down every step to making the perfect cheeseburger and was able to take completely untrained talent and quickly scale to a multibillion-dollar company.[1] SOPs are absolutely core to any thriving organization—family included. For my current company, I wrote a thirty-page handbook that outlines every role, task, and potential hurdle we have in the business. Over time, my team has broken it into even more documents that are job-specific across every function of our business—finance, customer service, product delivery, content creation, and so on.

The Benefits of SOPs

If everyone knows exactly what they are supposed to do and does it, you will have a higher quality output. And there are other benefits too:

- By mapping out each step in a process, you can save time and money by avoiding waste.
- Consistent processes mean consistent outcomes.
- A documented process is infinitely easier to learn than one you have to intuit, observe, or invent.
- When you clearly communicate exactly what you want and how you want it, you prevent the vast majority of corrections you'd otherwise need to make. Rather than "catching" people making mistakes and correcting them, put some foresight into what you want and explain it patiently. You'll have *way* more harmony in your relationships—work or family.
- A young kid (or young employee) can quickly be a contributing member of the team when they know exactly what to do and how to do it. As human beings, we all want to be part of a tribe; desiring to feel like an asset to the team is biologically wired into us. A checklist will provide a direct path to competency and contribution rather than putting that burden entirely on your young teammate.

Family SOPs

Even as I'm writing this, I know it sounds so corporate and jargony, and I'm sorry. I hope you will see that it really can help foster family harmony. Let me explain how we have created SOPs in our family and how they have helped us thrive.

The approach is simple: Create a checklist for whatever process you want members of your family to do. Chandler and I have SOPs for the kids regarding:

- Lunch pickup
- Bedtime routine
- Kitten care
- End-of-day pickup (four kids)
- Bathroom cleaning (three iterations)
- Morning chores (four kids)

We have also implemented similar SOPs for ourselves. A great example is our morning routine. Rather than tie it to the clock, we have a specific order of who makes coffee, who wakes the other, who works out, who showers, and so on. We've optimized it over time and gotten it on LOCK.

Each child can have their own SOPs, or you can have group SOPs for everyone. For example, here is our SOP for kids getting in the car:

Getting in the Car SOP

VIBE: Peaceful and Diligent

BUDDY TEAMS:

Team Blood	Everett	Truman
Team Panda	Charleston	Imogen
Team Kitty Cat	Penny	JoJo

CHECKLIST:

- ☐ Hair Brushed
- ☐ Teeth Brushed
- ☐ Clothes and Underwear
- ☐ Coat (or Sweatshirt)
- ☐ Appropriate Shoes On
- ☐ Buckled and Get Mint!

Access: Standard Operating Procedure (SOP) example titled Getting in the Car. The Vibe section says peaceful and diligent. There are three buddy teams, each with two kids. A checklist includes items such as Hair Brushed, Coat, and Appropriate Shoes, with related emojis.

As you can see, the checklist is really straightforward but also achievable for our children.

"Oh, if only it were that easy!" I hear you object. How do you get a child, especially a young one or a teen, to stick to the plan?

The "I Do, We Do, You Do" Approach

The real secret with SOPs is not in writing the document but in how you train the recipient. We've found the best training method for our kids is the "I do, we do, you do" approach.

"I Do"

When you have time to explain properly, take the kid and have them watch you do the SOP *exactly* how you want it done. Talk out loud as you do it and describe the details that matter to you.

"We Do"

Next, do the SOP together, talking through each step and encouraging your kid as they go. Again, do it with ample time and low stakes—you want this to feel more like practice than execution.

"You Do"

Finally, it is the kid's turn to demonstrate their knowledge. Watch them do the SOP in front of you, first with your coaching and eventually with you saying nothing as they explain each step. At this point, they are now fully competent in the SOP, and you can move to a place of accountability instead of training.

Before you start thinking that Chandler and I are freaks, I have to be honest: We're likely earning a B− in the training process. Sometimes we write up a checklist, tape it on the wall, and then get frustrated when nobody follows it. It's so easy to make lists, but it's much harder to train our children to follow them. However, when we've done this right, it has worked so well for our family! Our morning and end-of-day pickup routines have hugely blessed our family and removed some of our old stress points.

Tips for SOPs

- **Start slow.** One new SOP every other week is probably the most a kid can handle. It's better to train something incredibly well over a month versus dropping too much at one time and getting poor execution.
- **Emojis are your friends.** Making the SOP document look fun goes a long way. Adding emojis to demonstrate things, as well as using simple words, jokes, and so on, helps it not feel super corporate or cold.
- **Laminate your list and use dry-erase markers.** Who doesn't love crossing off items on a list? Laminating the checklist and attaching a dry-erase marker will do wonders for engaging the kids as they go. (Fair warning: We have to attach our markers with string, like pens at the bank. Otherwise, they'll wander off somewhere.)
- **Celebrate!** When a kid completes their job—especially the first couple of times—you have to celebrate with them. It's not just about giving them a reward; it's about letting them experience the great feeling of a job well done. The first time our oldest mowed the lawn by himself, I brought lemonade to him at the end, and as we looked at the yard, we basked in his job well done.

I hope you give this a shot for just one process. I've found that, over time, SOPs remove the need for nagging and pestering and keep everyone clear and on the same page.

> Standard Operating Procedures are one of those tools that, once you know how to use them well, you'll wonder how you ever functioned without them. You will be blown away at how capable your kids are and so surprised how even the youngest kids can learn complex processes. Children are born with an innate desire to help but without the skills or training. SOPs give them age-appropriate training so they *can* be helpful and feel the satisfaction of being a needed part of your family team. When you train your kids to be capable teammates, you'll be surprised at how your feelings change toward them. Instead of tiny people who are taking from you constantly, they are tiny people you can rely on. When our two-year-old has dressed herself, our five-year-old has cleaned her room, our seven-year-old has emptied the dishwasher, our nine-year-old has started a load of laundry, our eleven-year-old has made eggs, and our thirteen-year-old has fed the outdoor animals—all before we calmly sit down together for breakfast—I wonder how I could ever manage without them. They feel invested in the family because they were designed to be contributing members, and SOPs make it possible for them to tangibly help and bless the entire family.

ACTION PLAN

Simplify family routines with SOPs that everyone can follow.

- Pick one routine and jot down a checklist for it.
- Train your kids using "I Do, We Do, You Do" so they really get it.
- Make it fun—throw in some emojis, laminate it, use dry-erase markers, and definitely celebrate when they succeed.

CHAPTER 17

Organize Family Finances

Financials are the lifeblood of an organization. The person in charge of finances is intimately aware of every area of the business—always looking to invest in what drives the organization forward and cutting anything that is unnecessary. Rather than being an outside participant looming with a spreadsheet in hand, a good head of finance is an extension of each department—interviewing, understanding, projecting, and optimizing for maximum impact. They aren't just "no" people; they are collaborative brainstormers and inventors. Because, at the end of the day, they want to see the organization grow and thrive.

Too often, in both startups and households, we see the head of finance (the CFO) as this big bad wolf rather than an incredible resource, problem-solver, and confidant.

I was the head of finance for a startup before starting my own. I was twenty-five, and I learned a ton. Here were the four main functions of my role:

1. **Financial preparation.** Financial clarity is fundamental to making good decisions. This takes some technical (in

spreadsheets or accounting software) and communication skills to walk often nontechnical people through the results.

2. **Cost management.** When most people think of a head of finance, this is what they think of. And guess what? It's a huge deal. Having someone who is constantly reassessing what is actually necessary to an organization is a huge help.
3. **Morale and support.** Being the head of finance gives you unprecedented proximity to every area of the business. The CFO may see things that literally no one else in the organization sees. This gives you a great opportunity to connect, encourage, and help.
4. **Strategic insight.** You have a rare perspective because you work with all departments in the organization (procurement, sales, HR, and so on). That means you can speak to how each of these areas interacts and eliminate duplication.

Get to Know Your Expenses

As a family, you have to face your expenses together and review them regularly. Go through all your expenses and break them into the following categories:

- **Recurring expenses.** These are predictable expenses that don't really vary from month to month—things like your mortgage, cell phone bill, 529 contributions, and utilities.
- **Big expenses.** These are unpredictable expenses that you know are probably coming in this next year. Examples include travel/vacation, house maintenance, and car maintenance.
- **Giving expenses.** Charitable donations and acts of generosity go here.

- **Discretionary expenses (one for each parent).** Discretionary spending is the money you can control on a monthly basis—groceries, gas, gifts, clothing, and so on.

Now, average your spending in each of these categories across the past ninety days and add 10 percent. That should give you an idea of your family's monthly spending in each category.

Create Your Accounts

I want to talk about toothpaste. In his book *Profit First*, Mike Michalowicz talks about budgeting and "Why Your Business Is Like a Tube of Toothpaste."[1] Have you ever noticed that when you get a new tube of toothpaste, you'll glob a heaping pile onto your toothbrush, but toward the end, you can make do with a tiny amount squeezed out over several weeks?

This is accurate for our budgets as well. When our balances feel "full," we're loose with our money, but when they start feeling "empty," we suddenly become incredibly resourceful at doing more with less. This is so true in many families.

The main idea behind budgeting this way is to intentionally remove any excess from view—that way, you are always trying to do more with less.

I recommend using a bank that offers unlimited checking accounts at no cost. (Some banks limit you at three or four.) You will need a few accounts to help you get organized:

1. Income account for all income (no credit card or checks for this account)
2. Recurring payments account
3. Giving account
4. Spouse #1 discretionary expenses
5. Spouse #2 discretionary expenses

6. Savings account (separate bank; out of sight so it takes intention to access)

Name the accounts with the titles above and then put the amount you will transfer each month in parentheses behind it. For example:

- Income Account
- Recurring Expenses ($5,000)
- Big Expenses ($2,000)
- Giving (x%)
- Discretionary Expenses Spouse 1 ($2,000)
- Discretionary Expenses Spouse 2 ($1,000)

By naming them this way, you don't even have to look at a spreadsheet when it is time to transfer funds—you can just move the money based on the account title.

Connect Everything (and Review Outgoing)

This is the onetime pain: You need to connect all your auto-deposit accounts to your Income Account and then connect all your auto-pay expenses to their appropriate accounts. (I actually kind of love doing this exercise because it's a purge on any recurring expenses.)

I recommend ripping off the proverbial Band-Aid by setting up this system and then canceling the cards you used to use to pay for everything. Do your best to reconnect everything, but inevitably you'll forget some things. Once you start getting late notices or rejection notices in your email, it's a great time to ask yourself if you really need this thing you couldn't even remember. (Obviously, don't skip a mortgage or car payment. Hopefully, that's a given.)

Move Money Monthly

Set a calendar appointment each month for thirty minutes to distribute the money across the necessary accounts. Place whatever is left into investments or savings.

For example, on the first of each month you may have your paycheck and some rental or other business income in the Income Account. From there, fill each of the other expense accounts based on the amounts you've averaged. If there's anything left over, you can put it in savings or investment accounts far away.

This guarantees you'll never overspend on any category, and it encourages you to get creative to stay within your budget.

Optimize Every Ninety Days

Every ninety days, at your quarterly off-site, look at your accounts, review your quarterly goals, and adjust the amounts accordingly. If you have a big expense you need to make, you can make an adjustment in your budget paired with your goal. Or, if you need to trim back, you can do the analysis, cancel any recurring payment if necessary, and reset the bills. The most important first step is to live a few months in the system before you start trimming the budget. A good rule of thumb is to never change your budgeted amount by more than 5–10 percent if you want it to stick. If you think you can do more, go for it, but don't change the amount right away. Let it build up a balance, and then finalize it next quarter.

Benefits of Account-Based Budgeting

Chandler and I have managed our budget like this for quite some time, and we've found some really big benefits to doing it this way:

- **No categorization.** I hate categorizing transactions for our budget. It's tedious, and it's looking backward. What's great with this system is that after you do a onetime analysis, you never have to categorize anything again.

- **Easy to gauge.** In our weekly meeting, I can pull up our bank app and immediately see if something needs to change. If the balance is getting low in my discretionary account, I know I need to pull back for the rest of the month.
- **Forced creativity.** I've found I'm the most creative when I feel a little bit poor. If I have access to all our funds, I'm far more likely to buy things I don't need rather than think of creative ways to go without.
- **Control.** For my discretionary budget, I have total discretion. The same is true for Chandler and her discretionary budget. We've found that when we each control small subsets of our money, we do a better job of managing it overall. For example, Chandler might cut back on her expenses because she wants to save for something else, but a joint account could create a situation where I make a larger expense and unintentionally wipe out her savings. By giving each of us individual control, we use our money more effectively.

Kids and Money

Every week for the past year, we have paid our kids a generous allowance (completely separate from any chores). We believe the best way to teach our kids to steward assets is to give them assets early and coach them through poor decisions. So we pay each kid $1 per week for every year old they are (e.g., twelve years old = $12 per week).

These are my observations so far:

1. There's been zero change in work ethic since we've separated chore performance from money.

2. Everyone spent like crazy initially, but they have slowly changed to saving more and considering their purchases.
3. Kids have made some great decisions (buying assets, giving, paying for friends to do experiences) and some less-great decisions (spending $20 at the trampoline park on arcade games and cheap toys).
4. When they beg me to buy things or take everyone out to eat, I now ask them to pay, which puts it in perspective.
5. The number one perk to this whole thing is I'm seeing my kids learn to be *generous* toward each other and friends, especially for birthdays/holidays. I love seeing how they make decisions to share their abundance with others.

Two things I like about this system: It's promoting helpful conversations around money earlier, and it's setting them up well to steward our family's resources together.

ACTION PLAN

Here's how to get a simple, organized system for family finances up and running:

- Set up separate accounts for recurring expenses, big expenses, giving, and discretionary expenses.
- Transfer a set amount to each account at the start of every month.
- Review balances monthly and adjust amounts every quarter as needed.

CHAPTER 18

Create Family Traditions and Events

Culture is one of those buzzwords in startups that has become so overused. But beyond inspirational posters on walls, graffiti decorations, kombucha on tap, Ping-Pong tables, and nap pods (yes, nap pods), an effective culture is the top point of leverage any company can have. It's no exaggeration that if you figure out the right culture, everything else can work out.

Why? If you have a culture that attracts high-performing people, repels toxic people, and facilitates open communication and a sharing of the upside, then the best in the world will flock to your business. When that happens, they'll figure out how to grow the company. That's why corporations like Google spend heavily on culture and employee benefits like free meals, fitness centers, and on-campus amenities—all designed to enhance employee satisfaction and contribute to a positive culture.[1] A 2021 Bloomberg report estimated these expenses for Google's parent company, Alphabet Inc., to be $1 billion *annually*.[2] Whoa! (For reference, this is comparable to estimates of Google's investments in flagship projects like the Pixel smartphone.)

This maps back to family. Every person wants to know they belong to a thriving group of people with whom they feel safe and proud to be associated. It's a deep source of meaning for all humans, starting at an early age.

Celebrating Your Wins

The most impactful and widely used tool (and the highest leverage move you can make) for building a strong culture is to regularly bring the team together to celebrate "wins" and recognize each other's contributions. This goes by many names, but here are some examples:

1. All-Hands Meetings (Airbnb, Google): The entire company gathers weekly to discuss updates, celebrate wins, and align on goals.
2. Friday Demos (Stripe): Teams present what they've been working on throughout the week, fostering transparency and collaboration.
3. Weekly Show and Tell (Dropbox): Employees share new ideas, projects, or achievements, promoting a culture of creativity and recognition.
4. Town Halls and Kudos (Gusto): During a weekly town hall–style meeting, employees publicly acknowledge and thank their colleagues for their contributions.
5. Team Lunches (LinkedIn): Weekly lunches build cross-departmental relationships and encourage open communication in a relaxed setting.
6. Waffle Wednesdays (Facebook): This is a tradition where employees enjoy waffles together, fostering a sense of community.

7. Weekly Wins (HubSpot): Teams share their successes of the week in a companywide meeting, reinforcing positive momentum and celebrating achievements.
8. Learning Sessions (Atlassian): During weekly learning sessions, employees can teach or learn about new topics, promoting continuous learning and growth.
9. Open Mic Fridays (Spotify): Employees are invited to share their music, poetry, or other talents in a casual setting, encouraging creativity and self-expression.
10. Beer and Feedback Fridays (Buffer): During this casual Friday event, employees share a drink and give feedback on the company's progress, enhancing transparency and camaraderie.

Over the eight years I ran Cladwell.com, we did a couple iterations of weekly culture traditions. The first was called "Free Food Family Fridays." As you can probably surmise, we invited everyone on the team and their families to come into the office and share a lunch together. Some of my sweetest memories from the early days of the startup were seeing all the spouses and young kids gathering together. It created a community of authenticity and camaraderie unlike anything I've been a part of before or since. We ended up pausing it once we divided our team onto two coasts, but it was something really special.

We humans are tribal creatures. Traditions and ceremonies like this are deeply meaningful. There is deep relational and even spiritual significance in regularly celebrating together.

Your Family Weekly Celebration Dinner

One of the easiest ways to bring this into your family is the weekly celebration dinner. It might just be the most revolutionary tool in this entire book. It will have profound effects on the culture and cadence of your family. In Silicon Valley, these are called Celebration

Dinners. In Jewish culture, Shabbat Dinner. Growing up in the South, we called it Sunday Dinner (never mind that it occurred at 2 p.m.). In New York, you might call it Besties Brunch.

No matter the title, the formula is the same: Once a week, on the same day each week, you gather as a family, look each other in the eye, raise a glass, and celebrate the good things in your life and the amazing people you get to share them with.

Here's the process:

1. **Gather every week.** It's fairly easy to start but incredibly difficult to maintain. Pick a day of the week to have a meal as a family and then make sure you always do it. I think making it a nonnegotiable is what creates its cultural value. If, no matter what, you always do your family dinner, that says to your family—and the world—that this organization exists, has its own identity, and is more important than every other organization trying to pull it apart.

   Through birthday parties, sports events, travel, tiredness, work emergencies, and on and on, the world will try to keep you from consistently meeting together as a family every week. The harder you push for it, the stronger you communicate to your family that this thing matters.

   For us, even if we are traveling, we try to at least take a minute as a family at a restaurant or a friend's house to pause, look around the table, and acknowledge that this is our weekly celebration. Regularity and priority are the keys to that depth.

2. **Have a special meal.** We humans are embodied creatures. Taste, smell, touch, sight, and sound all map to memory and meaning in a way we still don't fully understand. That's why the celebratory dinner needs to be set apart in the senses.

   We put more effort into the food of our celebratory meal. It's the best meal of the week—steak, spaghetti and meatballs, tons of bread and olive oil, and so on. It's something we don't have every single night. We also have a special dessert, something our kids really look forward to.

Chandler lights a candle during our weekly celebratory dinner. Nine out of ten times, one of our kids blows it out and sprays wax on the table, but I guess that's a sensory experience too. The rest of the week, we're (obviously) not that fancy, so the smells of the candle and the food communicate to our kids that it's a special time. My hope is that when they are in their thirties and come over on a Friday night, they will feel transported immediately to a place of joy and safety.

We also create a special atmosphere by using a tablecloth, adding flowers, and making the whole setting look great. Again, this is not the norm for us, so it sets this meal apart, signaling that the celebratory dinner is different. You can choose some music or even sing, if that's your thing. We also make an effort to wear nicer clothes—no sweats or clothes from yard work. All these things are hooks in our family's minds to set this meal apart as a tradition tied to who we are and what we're like.

3. **Express gratitude.** The question of how often to "celebrate" is a regular discussion with startup founders. Sometimes it feels too soon to celebrate—because things might go wrong—but by the time it feels "safe," it's already old news. The solution is to celebrate regularly.

   At the celebration dinner, a key part is to look at your family life—your health, your relationships, your finances, your efforts—and be grateful together. We all know the studies that show gratitude maps to happiness, and experientially, I can confirm it's true.[3] There is something truly magical about looking each person in your family in the eye and saying, "Look at this incredible life we've been given." It creates at least a temporary finish line for everyone to say, "Wow, we have enough."

We can always do more, have more, and perform more, but it needs to come from a place of gratitude rather than saying, "I'll only be grateful when x happens."

Our family has gone through rough points of financial lack, death, and chaos, but we've never skipped a celebration meal. I think that's a big reason why we've banded together through it all. Despite all those obstacles, we always have something to be thankful for.

4. **Celebrate one another.** In a startup, celebrating one another means recognizing achievements or living up to the company's values. In a family, it means speaking what is or what you hope to be true about your children and spouse.

   At our family celebration dinner, I read a short passage from King Solomon that praises his wife (or mother?—the interpretation isn't entirely clear). It ends with this: "Her children rise up and call her blessed; her husband also, and he praises her: 'Many women have done excellently, but you surpass them all'" (Prov. 31:28–29 ESV). At that point, the kids and I stand up and cheer for my wife for a week well done. It is SO powerful to praise your spouse in front of the family. If you don't ascribe to a particular faith, simply take this moment to compliment your partner in your own words.

   Then Chandler and I speak a few words about our sons and daughters, saying what we see as true or hope to be true about their character. Sometimes it's silly or cheesy. Sometimes it's deep. But I know I've never heard of anyone who wishes their parents didn't speak more life-giving words over them. This gives me an occasion to do it each week.

Watch Out

- Don't feel you have to set the bar too high. It's *totally* fine to order pizza, use paper plates, and say cheers to a good week. Start small—even a small effort will have a huge effect. Don't let perfection be the enemy of the good.

- Life is going to get in the way. Stuff will come up. Like I said, you have to stay committed. I also realize that if you are going to be part of an extended community (neighborhood, sports team, faith group, extended family, and so forth), it means compromising from time to time. My general rule is if we start to miss more than one in four celebration dinners, something needs to be systemically addressed. If we're making three out of four, I'm okay with the children going to the occasional birthday party or sports game or whatever.
- Part of being the leader is doing the awkward thing, even when everyone thinks it's lame. Just stick with it.
- You might be surprised to hear this, but babies don't really enjoy long, formal, meaningful dinners. They also tend to vocally express their dislike of these environments. For those of us with babies, toddlers, teenagers, or, frankly, just kids of any age, this will not be the magical moment we have in our imagination. When we're old, it will be magical in our memory, but for now, just set your expectations accordingly: The two-year-old will freak out because you won't let them hold the sharp knife; the four-year-old will want to go play after two minutes; the seven-year-old will occasionally burp so loudly the silverware shakes; the ten-year-old will roll their eyes or say something cutting to a sibling; and the twelve-year-old won't stop correcting their sibling for eating with their mouth open. All in one meal. You can still be grateful and laugh in the midst of it.

I simply cannot recommend this tool enough. It will fundamentally change the direction and culture of your family. If you're ever in Cincinnati and want to stop by and visit our weekly family celebration, shoot me a message. I'd love to share the experience with you.

> The memories and traditions that will stick with our kids for a lifetime are the ones paired with rich experiences. During our weekly celebratory dinners, Blake and I take on different roles. He leans into a "master of ceremonies" role, explaining to our kids and any guests present what we're doing and why we're doing it. He leads the conversation, and what he communicates in words, I communicate through all the other senses. I prepare really good food, set the mood with music, dim the lights, and make things cozy. The smell of Friday night meatballs simmering on the stove, the flickering of candles on the table, and the soft atmosphere will drive these memories deep into our souls. A sensory experience without leadership is just a nice meal, but a talk from one parent without the embodied experience falls flat and isn't memorable. Lean in to your gifts and work with your partner to bring the best of what you can both offer to the table.

ACTION PLAN

Here's how to start a weekly family celebration dinner that brings everyone together and builds lasting traditions:

- Pick a consistent day each week and make this meal a non-negotiable family event.
- Prepare a special meal, add a few extra touches to set the mood, and make it memorable.
- Take time to express gratitude and celebrate each other, sharing wins from the week.

CHAPTER 19

Move Forward Together

6:00 A.M. PST, SEPTEMBER 12, 2018

My phone alarm went off in my Venice Beach Airbnb. I was pretty jet-lagged and dreading the day's fundraising meetings. As I grabbed my phone, I saw a text message from Chandler:

> Hey, I'm having some heavy bleeding and the OB/GYN told me to come in. Please call me.

I remember my first boss telling me war stories about his investment banking years—how he would stay up thirty-six hours straight to get a deal done, sleep in the limo, and change in the office. He once told me about a time when his wife was miscarrying in the middle of a deal. He didn't come home, and he said it almost destroyed their marriage. That story played in the back of my head, and I texted her back:

> I'm coming home.

I packed my bags, got an Uber to the airport, canceled the day's meetings, and called Chandler. I tried to convince her that we didn't have to get sad yet. "Let's just process this as it comes and not project the worst-case scenario," I said.

I'm pretty good at holding out hope, but there was a feeling of inevitability. LA to Cincinnati is a long haul, so I journaled, prayed, worked, and tried to escape any negative feelings by watching movies (my signature move).

I arrived at 5 p.m. EST, ran through the airport, ran to the Uber, ran from the Uber into the house, and ran upstairs. The moment Chandler saw me, we both started crying and hugging each other. Penny, our three-year-old, informed me bluntly: "Today's a sad day. Our baby died."

We'd never really had a loss with our family of six before. You never know how your family will react until it happens.

I was a little confused. Yes, I was sad, but was I as sad as if my one-year-old had died? No. It's not that our baby wasn't a person—it's just that she wasn't as much of a person as my children I'd held. I felt guilty for my reaction. In the end, I decided it was best to just lean in and allow myself to imagine the full personhood of my daughter; this allowed me to get through it better than if I kept analyzing my reactions.

Chandler and I, along with our kids ages seven, five, three, and one, dove into the sadness of losing our baby. We named her Vera Lesa. *Vera* means "faith"—it seemed like the only solution at the time was to trust that God can take sad things and make them beautiful. *Lesa* means "consecrated to God"—as the only other action we felt we could take was to surrender to whatever was happening. I had recently read the book of Job, and I felt like we could trust that (a) this pain was not our fault, (b) God always has a plan, and (c) we likely wouldn't see its full meaning in this life.

We mourned Vera. The kids, Chandler, and I wrote letters to her about the life we'd looked forward to sharing with her. We imagined the major life milestones we would have celebrated—learning to walk, reading, driving, graduating, getting married, having children and grandchildren. We apologized for anything we had ever felt, thought, or said against her. We expressed truths we wanted her to know. The kids mostly drew pictures; Chandler and I wrote. And wrote. And wrote.

In mourning Vera, we might have sung a song (I can't remember). I've never seen my dad cry, so I don't really know what impact that has on kids—but whatever it is, my kids are going to feel it because I wept in front of my family and my children for the daughter I'd never know.

I'm telling you this story because it highlights the limitations of this book. There is no framework for certain family situations. In the end, we are a family—not a business. Not even an organization. We are a family. And death is something only a family can process together.

So, what is the use of this book then?

For me, bringing my operational skills home was the first step to bringing my heart fully home. As I've been writing this book, I keep picturing the dad in *The Sound of Music*, Captain von Trapp. Remember him? He ran his family like a military commander. I always thought he was kind of a jerk for making his kids march around and respond to a whistle. But it made sense—the guy fought in WWI. He knew how to lead a battalion, and he brought those skills home. His path of growth started with bringing what he had—a military skill set—home, but it didn't stop there. Over time, and with the help of his new wife, he expanded beyond his zone of safety—his skills—to bring his heart fully home.

This has been my experience as well. I think it may have been too big a jump for me to go from being fully invested in my work to coming home and being fully present and wholehearted. So the first step was to be competent in what I had—startup leadership—at home. But it didn't stop there. As I implemented these practices with my family, my little Grinchy heart expanded and connected to the amazing people who are a part of me. And when tragedy hit us, I could be fully present—physically, emotionally, spiritually—as a husband and father.

I want that for you too. And my hope is that bringing your full work self into your home might be the secret door to help you get there.

Tools aside for a second, what do you have?

Are you a teacher? Teach your family.

Are you a designer? Design a beautiful family.

Are you a general contractor? Build your family.

Whatever you have, I pray you will start with that—and that it becomes the first step in a journey for your heart to fully find rest in your home.

EPILOGUE

If you were looking for operational tactics to help you create order, teamwork, and vision for your family, that part of the book is now done.

Before I leave you, though, it would feel disingenuous not to acknowledge the foundation upon which I've discovered and built these systems: the narrative of family found in the Jewish law, prophets, and wisdom literature of the Old Testament, as well as the Christian New Testament.

I wanted to write this book based on my experience as a founder because I believe these principles are beneficial for human thriving, no matter the faith of those humans. However, my path to discovering this truth actually started with a sermon in a church and has been guided by fifteen years of studying the Bible with a group of fathers, exploring what it looks like to build a household organization.

To *not* share that framework with you would be "hiding the ball" and could put me in danger of taking credit for concepts that didn't originate with me. So, here is a brief overview.

In the book of Genesis, God starts by giving humans a mission to care for the earth, obey him, and expand into a fruitful family. Within two chapters, they fail this mission and chaos ensues. Murder. Strife. Natural disaster. War. Incest. Slavery. World confusion.

By chapter 12, the world is a mess. So, what is God's solution?

Does he establish a government? No. Does he found a nonprofit? No. A B-Corp? No. A startup with a strong mission? No. He calls a family.

Specifically, he calls a husband and wife, Abram and Sarai, who are incapable of having children. And he says to them:

> I will make of you a great nation, I will bless you, and I will make your name great; and you are to be a blessing. I will bless those who bless you, but I will curse anyone who curses you; and by you all the families of the earth will be blessed. (Gen. 12:2–3)

What transpires after this is the story of Abram, whom God renames Abraham ("father of many") as he builds his family, makes deals, goes to war, and blesses those he encounters. My favorite detail is that Abraham is a tribal leader—a king—but he never takes that title. When he goes to war with other nations, the text lists many kings by title:

> In the days of Amraphel king of Shinar, Arioch king of Ellasar, Chedorlaomer king of Elam, and Tidal king of Goiim, these kings made war with Bera king of Sodom, Birsha king of Gomorrah, Shinab king of Admah, Shemeber king of Zeboiim, and the king of Bela (that is, Zoar). (14:1–2 ESV)

And then the text just mentions "Abram the Hebrew" (v. 13). He needed no higher title than *father*. He serves as a prototypical father for Jews and Christians alike as he, though flawed, seeks to lead his family to bless others.

To be clear, I believe this is our call as micro-families: to team up multigenerationally and seek to bless the world.

In the biblical narrative, it doesn't stop with Abraham. That's why the Christian New Testament starts, in the book of Matthew, with a long genealogy: to demonstrate that Jesus Christ is directly in the lineage of this same family and to show that he is the fulfillment of God's promise to bless the earth, extending beyond the people of Israel to the entire world.

Whether you are a Christian or not, you need to come to grips with the fact that something happened in the first century AD that forever changed the earth. (I mean, we call it "the first century" for a reason.)

Until that point, domination, violence, and power ruled the earth. Women were property. Children were disposable. Foreigners were resources to be used up. But something happened when Jesus came. For the first time in human history, the concepts of dignity for all humans, human rights, and care for the marginalized began to spread throughout our planet. These concepts all came from Jesus, who came from the family of Abraham.

If you like hospitals, schools, universities, health care, charitable organizations, orphanages, social justice movements, the legal system, and, yes, family, then you are the beneficiary of this particular family's ambitious mission.

As a Christian—an "adopted" member of that family, as the apostle Paul mentions in Romans 8—I see it as my responsibility to lead my family in continuing the mission to be a blessing to all nations and to teach them to obey the ways of Jesus.

The early Christian church didn't meet in public buildings or even in religious buildings. It met in houses. The story of the early church—this early movement—took place in and through families and homes. I believe the church today is most effective when it continues this tradition.

This is my framework for life: to lead my family as part of a larger, global, multiethnic family mission to bless the world. It is the most meaningful organization I have ever been a part of, and

I would love for any person reading this book to at least consider the incredible adventure and joy that come with it.

Thank you for sticking with me through this whole book. I've never done anything like this before, and it's truly been one of the most enjoyable endeavors I've ever undertaken. I hope you can feel through these pages that I genuinely want this to be a blessing to you and your family for generations to come.

May you be a blessing to every family you come across, and may you feel God's pleasure as you do so.

ACKNOWLEDGMENTS

Families That Have Shaped Us

- **The Baer and Smith Families.** You chose to live counter-culturally by homeschooling us, faithfully providing for us, and involving us in great communities of faith. You took your faith seriously and encouraged us to do the same. We stand on your shoulders.
- **The Meurer Family.** Mitch and Shelly, you created a home where there was love for everyone and even some left over. I (Blake) needed that in high school more than you knew, and I want to do the same for others.
- **The Pryor Family.** Jeremy and April, so much of our family DNA comes from you. Thank you for mentoring us three-plus nights a week for almost a year, sitting on the board of our company, working with us, inviting us along on adventures, helping us through tough times, giving us a platform to teach, and, most of all, showing us what a beautiful family can look like.
- **The Peters Family.** Andrew and Rachel, thank you for inviting us into your family planning meetings for years, sharing your home with us, and showing us how fun family meetings can be.

You Would Not Have This Book in Your Hands Without

- **Chandler Allsmith.** I (Blake) know it's weird because we're coauthors, but I want to call out that Chandler was the one who said we have to do this. Chandler, I've spent the past twenty years striving to live up to what you see in me—I love you so much.
- **Chris Ridenour.** I was 50/50 on writing the book, and your recommendation tipped the scale. This ended up being one of the most enjoyable works of my life.
- **Taylor Brooks.** Your vision, encouragement, and generosity are the reason this is an actual book and not just a Google Doc. Thank you, thank you, thank you.

Beta Readers

To those who acted as "beta readers" for this book—thank you for putting up with how business-y the first draft was, for your helpful feedback, and for answering my ongoing texts asking for clarification and help:

Taylor Brooks
Julie Davis
Chris Marlin
Punit Shah
Landon Ellis
Austin Mock
Michelle Schneider
Ben Munoz
Aparna Pande
Lucas Cole
Cameron Akrami
Salem Molina
Kathryn Cradduck
Scott Keenan
Chris Kubik
Madeline Schmidt
Mark Tiderman
Tom Richards
Phil Cotnoir

Professionals

- **Becky Alexander** (first developmental edit): You did such a great job seeing what was good in the transcript and helping me meet readers where they are. Thank you.
- **Jenny Morgan** (first copyedit): You strike such a great balance in discerning which writing rules to obey and which to defy. Thanks for keeping my voice while making it sound way less dumb.
- **Dan Balow** (agent): Your wisdom and cool, calm, and collected manner have been great through this process. You are the consummate professional. Thanks for taking a swing on two authors with as many kids as we have Instagram followers.

FURTHER READING

I want to leave you with some recommendations for further reading on a few different topics, depending on which areas might interest you.

Team Culture and Communication

The Culture Code: The Secrets of Highly Successful Groups by Daniel Coyle (Bantam Books, 2018)

The Five Dysfunctions of a Team: A Leadership Fable by Patrick Lencioni (Jossey-Bass, 2002)

Nonviolent Communication: A Language of Life by Marshall B. Rosenberg (PuddleDancer Press, 2015)

Start with Why: How Great Leaders Inspire Everyone to Take Action by Simon Sinek (Portfolio/Penguin, 2011)

Leadership Development

The Four Obsessions of an Extraordinary Executive: A Leadership Fable by Patrick Lencioni (Jossey-Bass, 2000)

Leadership and Self-Deception: Getting Out of the Box by The Arbinger Institute (Berrett-Koehler Publishers, Inc., 2002)

On Becoming a Leader by Warren Bennis (Basic Books, 2009)

Radical Candor: Be a Kick-Ass Boss Without Losing Your Humanity by Kim Scott (St. Martin's Press, 2019)

Traction: Get a Grip on Your Business by Gino Wickman (BenBella Books, 2012)

Wooden on Leadership: How to Create a Winning Organization by John Wooden and Steve Jamison (McGraw Hill, 2005)

The Biblical Role of Family

Abraham's Wallet, www.abrahamswallet.com

Family Revision: How Ancient Wisdom Can Heal the Modern Family by Jeremy Pryor (Family Teams, 2019)

Family Teams, www.familyteams.com

Making Disciples in and Through Your Home

1 KH, www.1KH.org

Historic Impact of Christianity

Dominion by Tom Holland (Basic Books, 2019)

The Case for God and Jesus

The Reason for God by Tim Keller (Penguin Books, 2009)

NOTES

Chapter 1 The Power of a Framework

1. John Hunter, "W. Edwards Deming Quote: A Bad System Will Beat a Good Person Every Time," The Deming Institute, February 26, 2015, https://deming.org/a-bad-system-will-beat-a-good-person-every-time/.

2. Wendell Berry, *The Art of the Commonplace: The Agrarian Essays of Wendell Berry*, ed. Norman Wirzba (Counterpoint, 2002), 64.

3. Erin Griffith, "Honey, I Love You. Didn't You See My Slack About It?" *The New York Times*, May 12, 2024, www.nytimes.com/2024/05/12/business/relationships-trello-slack-notion.html.

4. Stephen R. Covey, *The 7 Habits of Highly Effective Families* (Golden Books, 1997), 72.

5. Jean M. Twenge and W. Keith Campbell, "Cultural Individualism Is Linked to Later Onset of Adult-Role Responsibilities Across Time and Regions," *Journal of Cross-Cultural Psychology* 49, no. 4 (2018): 673–83, https://journals.sagepub.com/doi/10.1177/0022022118764838.

6. Jeremy Pryor, *Family Revision: How Ancient Wisdom Can Heal the Modern Family* (Family Teams, 2014), 25.

AREA 1 Relationships

1. "Divorce Rate by State 2025," World Population Review, accessed October 2, 2025, https://worldpopulationreview.com/state-rankings/divorce-rate-by-state.

2. Gary Burnison, "7 Years Ago, Google Set Out to Find What Makes the 'Perfect' Team—and What They Found Shocked Other Researchers," CNBC, September 13, 2019, www.cnbc.com/2019/02/28/what-google-learned-in-its-quest-to-build-the-perfect-team.html. See also Charles Duhigg, "What Google Learned from Its Quest to Build the Perfect Team," *The New York Times*, February 25,

2016, www.nytimes.com/2016/02/28/magazine/what-google-learned-from-its-quest-to-build-the-perfect-team.html.

3. Julia Pugachevsky, "Young, Successful Tech Cofounders Have a Secret Weapon: Couples Therapy," *Business Insider*, April 18, 2024, www.businessinsider.com/young-successful-tech-cofounders-couples-therapy-2024-4. See also Arielle Pardes, "The Pandemic Drives Cofounders to Couples Therapy," *WIRED*, August 4, 2021, www.wired.com/story/startup-cofounders-couples-therapy-silicon-valley/.

Chapter 2 Start with a Weekly Date Night

1. Allison Daminger, "The Cognitive Dimension of Household Labor," *American Sociological Review* 84, no. 4 (2019): 609–33.

Chapter 4 Who's the CEO?

1. Marc A. Feigen, Michael Jenkins, and Anton Warendh, "Is It Time to Consider Co-CEOs?" *Harvard Business Review*, July 1, 2022, https://hbsp.harvard.edu/product/S22042-PDF-ENG. See also Meghan Walsh, "Are Two Heads Better Than One?" *Briefings*, September 29, 2022, www.kornferry.com/insights/briefings-magazine/issue-56/are-two-heads-better-than-one.

2. Duhigg, "What Google Learned from Its Quest to Build the Perfect Team."

Chapter 5 Where to Handle Disagreements

1. Kim Scott, *Radical Candor: Be a Kick-Ass Boss Without Losing Your Humanity* (St. Martin's Press, 2019).

2. Dan Senor and Saul Singer, *Start-Up Nation: The Story of Israel's Economic Miracle* (Twelve, 2009), 8.

Chapter 6 How to Handle Disagreements

1. "Amazon Memo: What Lessons Does It Hold?," Management Consulted, September 11, 2024, https://managementconsulted.com/amazon-memo/.

2. The Arbinger Institute, *Leadership and Self-Deception: Getting Out of the Box*, 2nd edition (Berrett-Koehler, 2015).

AREA 2 Direction

1. Deloitte Insights, "2020 Global Marketing Trends," pdf, accessed October 8, 2025, www.marketersbyadlatina.com/uploads/files/-2214-2020-global-marketing-trends.pdf.

2. Deloitte Insights, "2020 Global Marketing Trends," 10.

3. Associated Press, "Biggs Has Plans for Tyson," *Oroville Mercury-Register*, August 19, 1987, 1B, col. 2.

Chapter 7 Define Your Family Values

1. Phil Knight, *Shoe Dog: A Memoir by the Creator of Nike* (Scribner, 2016), 224.

2. Gino Wickman, *Traction: Get a Grip on Your Business* (BenBella Books, 2011), 172.

Chapter 8 Craft Your Family Mission

1. Ian D. Boreham and Nicola S. Schutte, "The Relationship Between Purpose in Life and Depression and Anxiety: A Meta-Analysis," *Journal of Clinical Psychology* 79, no. 12 (2023): 2736–67, https://doi.org/10.1002/jclp.23576.

Chapter 9 Cast a Vision for the Future

1. See Mike Breen and Ben Sternke, *Oikonomics: How to Invest in Life's Five Capitals the Way Jesus Did* (3dm International, 2015).

Chapter 10 Set Meaningful Family Goals

1. George T. Doran, "There's a S.M.A.R.T. Way to Write Management's Goals and Objectives," *Management Review* 70, no. 11 (1981): 35–36.

Chapter 11 The Daily Stand-Up

1. Ken Schwaber and Jeff Sutherland, "The Scrum Guide," pdf, November 2017, https://scrumguides.org/docs/scrumguide/v2017/2017-Scrum-Guide-US.pdf.

Chapter 12 The Weekly Meeting

1. "John Cleese on Creativity in Management," YouTube video, 36:59, posted June 21, 2017, by Video Arts, https://youtu.be/Pb5oIIPO62g?si=xiOwzkqAs6MrGDNj.

Chapter 14 The Annual Retreat

1. Daniel H. Pink, *When: The Scientific Secrets of Perfect Timing* (Riverhead Books, 2018), chapter 3.

Chapter 15 Build a Weekly Rhythm for Family Flow

1. Stephen R. Covey, A. Roger Merrill, and Rebecca R. Merrill, *First Things First* (Free Press, 1996), 88.

Chapter 16 Streamline Routines with SOPs

1. "How to Think in Systems (and Why McDonald's Has a University)," Frontera, January 31, 2023, https://fronterabrands.com/systems-thinking.

Chapter 17 Organize Family Finances

1. Mike Michalowicz, *Profit First* (Portfolio Penguin, 2017), 39–40.

Chapter 18 Create Family Traditions and Events

1. See Forbes Technology Council, "13 Reasons Google Deserves Its 'Best Company Culture' Award," *Forbes*, February 8, 2018, www.forbes.com/sites/forbestechcouncil/2018/02/08/13-reasons-google-deserves-its-best-company-culture-award/.

2. Yaël Bizouati-Kennedy, "Google Is Saving over $1 Billion Thanks to Work from Home," Yahoo! Finance, April 30, 2021, https://finance.yahoo.com/news/google-saving-over-1-billion-171650216.html.

3. For example, see Maureen Salamon, "Gratitude Enhances Health, Brings Happiness—and May Even Lengthen Lives," *Harvard Health Publishing*, September 11, 2024, www.health.harvard.edu/blog/gratitude-enhances-health-brings-happiness-and-may-even-lengthen-lives-202409113071.

BLAKE AND CHANDLER ALLSMITH are entrepreneurs, investors, and parents of seven children thirteen and under (as of 2025). They live on fourteen acres along the banks of the Ohio River in Northern Kentucky, where their home feels a little like a startup and a little like a summer camp.

Blake served as CEO of Cladwell.com for eight years, leading the company through its growth and eventual sale in 2019. He now advises founders through his agency Allsmith.org, as well as through Techstars, 500 Startups, and a venture capital firm where he serves as entrepreneur-in-residence.

Chandler homeschools their kids, manages their rental properties, and homesteads "for fun." She also hosts *The Best Homeschool Podcast Ever*.

Together, they create resources at TheAllsmiths.com to help families move from chaos to clarity—applying entrepreneurial frameworks in a way that's equal parts practical and story-driven, with plenty of humor about the messiness of real life.

Rooted in their Christian faith, the Allsmiths believe family is God's primary institution for changing the world. Their work is grounded in grace, structure, and a long-term view. Their family mission is simple: **Enter for Refuge. Go Out and Restore. All in Love.** They hope to help others build households where that kind of life is possible.

CONNECT WITH BLAKE AND CHANDLER:

TheAllsmiths.com